ALEXANDER-GRACE EDUCATION

MW01489454

CONTENTS

ALEXANDER-GRACE EDUCATION

Understanding the MAP Tests

The NWEA MAP (Measures of Academic Progress) test is an adaptive assessment that is designed to measure student growth and progress in a variety of subject areas. The test is taken by millions of students across the United States and is widely used by educators to help inform instruction and measure student outcomes. The NWEA MAP test is administered online and provides immediate feedback on student performance, allowing teachers to adjust their teaching strategies and provide targeted support to individual students.

The NWEA MAP test is unique in that it is adaptive, which means that the difficulty of the questions adjusts based on the student's responses. This allows the test to be more personalized to each student's abilities and provides a more accurate measure of their knowledge and skills. The test covers a range of subject areas, including mathematics, reading, language usage, and science, and is administered multiple times throughout the school year. This allows teachers to track student progress and growth over time and make data-driven decisions to improve student outcomes.

Purpose and Benefits of MAP Testing

The primary purpose of the MAP Test is to provide valuable insights into a student's learning and academic progress. By offering a detailed analysis of a student's performance in reading, language usage, mathematics, and science, the test helps teachers tailor their instruction to meet individual needs. The MAP Test also serves as a benchmarking tool, allowing schools and districts to compare their students' performance with national norms and other local institutions.

This data-driven approach enables educators to make informed decisions about curriculum, instructional methods, and resource allocation, ultimately leading to improved student outcomes. Additionally, the MAP Test can help identify gifted students who may benefit from advanced or accelerated programs, as well as students who may require additional support or interventions.

Test Format and Content

The MAP Test is divided into four primary content areas: reading, language usage, mathematics, and science. Each section consists of multiple-choice questions that cover various topics and skills within the respective subject. The test is untimed, allowing students to work at their own pace and ensuring a lower level of test anxiety. The computer-adaptive nature of the MAP Test ensures that the difficulty of questions adjusts based on a student's performance, making it suitable for students of all ability levels. As a result, the MAP Test not only evaluates a student's mastery of grade-level content but also assesses their readiness for more advanced material.

Adaptive Testing and Scoring System

One of the unique aspects of the MAP Test is its adaptive testing system. As students answer questions, the test adjusts the difficulty of subsequent questions based on their performance. This adaptive nature allows the test to home in on a student's true ability level, providing more accurate and meaningful results. The MAP Test uses a RIT (Rasch Unit) scale to measure student achievement, which is an equal-interval scale that allows for easy comparison of scores across grade levels and subjects. This scoring system allows educators and parents to track a student's growth over time, making it an invaluable tool for understanding academic progress and setting individualized learning goals.

Preparing for Success on the MAP Test

Effective preparation for the MAP Test involves a combination of understanding the test format, mastering content knowledge, and developing test-taking strategies. This test prep book is designed to provide students with comprehensive guidance on each content area, offering targeted instruction and practice questions to build confidence and ensure success. Additionally, the book includes test-taking tips and strategies to help students approach the test with a calm and focused mindset. By working through this book and dedicating time to consistent practice, students will be well-equipped to excel on the MAP Test and achieve their academic goals.

Note that, since there is no cap to the level that a student can work to in preparation for this test, there is no 'completion' of content, as students can simply do questions from grades above in preparation. It should be noted that students are not expected to work far above grade level to succeed in this test, as consistent correct answers are more relevant.

What Is Contained Within this Book?

Within this book you will find 320 questions based off content which would be found within the MAP test your student will take. The content found in this book will be the equivalent of grade 4 level. Note that since this test is adaptive, some students may benefit by looking at several grade levels of content, not just their own.

At the end of the book will contain answers alongside explanations. It is recommended to look and check your answers thoroughly in regular intervals to make sure you improve as similar questions come up.

Topic 1 - Understanding Character Motivation

In a small, peaceful town, there lived a curious puppy named Max. Max loved to explore and often wandered around the neighborhood. One sunny day, Max followed a butterfly into a neighbor's garden, where he found a lonely old man sitting alone. The man, Mr. Jenkins, seemed sad. Max decided to keep him company. They quickly became friends. Max's visits brought joy to Mr. Jenkins, who started smiling more often. Max realized that his small act of kindness had a big impact.

1.1) Why did Max enter Mr. Jenkins' garden?

☐ To chase a butterfly

☐ To find food

☐ To play with toys

☐ To escape from home

1.2) How did Max feel about his adventures?

☐ Scared

☐ Excited

☐ Bored

☐ Tired

1.3) What did Max find in Mr. Jenkins' garden?

☐ A lonely old man

☐ A lost kitten

☐ A treasure chest

☐ A beautiful flower

ALEXANDER-GRACE EDUCATION

1.4) How did Mr. Jenkins feel before meeting Max?

☐ Sad

☐ Angry

☐ Happy

☐ Amused

1.5) What lesson does the story teach?

☐ Puppies are mischievous

☐ Kindness can bring joy

☐ Adventure is important

☐ Gardens are fun to explore

Lily was a creative girl who loved to draw and paint. Her class was assigned an art project, and Lily was determined to create something special. She decided to paint a mural of her neighborhood, showcasing the people and places she loved. While working on her mural, Lily discovered that she enjoyed capturing the beauty of everyday life. Her classmates were impressed by her talent and dedication. Lily felt proud and realized that through her art, she could share her unique perspective with others.

1.6) What was Lily's art project?

☐ A mural of her neighborhood

☐ A sculpture

☐ A landscape painting

☐ A self-portrait

ALEXANDER-GRACE EDUCATION

1.7) Why did Lily choose to paint her neighborhood?

☐ It was a school assignment

☐ It was easy to do

☐ She loved her community

☐ She couldn't think of anything else

1.8) How did Lily feel while working on her mural?

☐ Confused

☐ Indifferent

☐ Frustrated

☐ Proud

1.9) What did Lily's classmates think of her mural?

☐ It was too colorful

☐ They didn't care

☐ They were impressed

☐ It was unimpressive

1.10) What did Lily learn from doing the art project?

☐ She prefers math

☐ She can share her perspective through art

☐ Art is challenging

☐ Murals are difficult to paint

Tommy, a young boy with a great love for animals, found a hurt bird in his backyard. Carefully, he picked it up and made a small nest in a box. Every day, Tommy would feed the bird and watch over it. As the bird got better, it would chirp happily whenever Tommy was near. Finally, the day came when the bird was well enough to fly away. Tommy felt sad but knew it was the right thing to let the bird go free.

1.11) What did Tommy find in his backyard?

☐ A magic stone

☐ A hurt bird

☐ A lost puppy

☐ A hidden treasure

1.12) How did Tommy care for the bird?

☐ He fed it and watched over it

☐ He left it alone

☐ He played music for it

☐ He took it to a zoo

1.13) What change did Tommy notice as the bird recovered?

☐ It chirped happily

☐ It danced

☐ It stopped eating

☐ It painted pictures

1.14) How did Tommy feel when the bird left?

□ Extremely happy

□ Angry and upset

□ Indifferent

□ Sad but understanding

1.15) Why did Tommy let the bird go?

□ Because it was well enough to fly

□ Because it was magical

□ Because he was bored of it

□ Because his parents told him to

Sara loved spending time with her grandmother, who told the best stories. One day, her grandmother told her about a secret garden hidden behind their house. Filled with curiosity, Sara decided to find it. After searching for hours, she found a beautiful garden full of colorful flowers and singing birds. Sara realized the stories her grandmother told were not just tales, but real adventures waiting to be discovered.

1.16) Who did Sara enjoy listening to?

□ Her teacher

□ Her grandmother

□ Her best friend

□ A famous explorer

1.17) What did Sara's grandmother tell her about?

☐ A hidden treasure

☐ An ancient castle

☐ A magical forest

☐ A secret garden

1.18) What motivated Sara to search for the garden?

☐ Her friends' encouragement

☐ A map she found

☐ Curiosity and love for adventure

☐ A school assignment

1.19) What did Sara find?

☐ An old, abandoned house

☐ A hidden treasure chest

☐ A garden with colorful flowers and birds

☐ A magical creature

1.20) What did Sara learn from this experience?

☐ Exploring can be scary

☐ Stories can be real adventures

☐ Birds are fascinating

☐ Gardening is fun

In a bustling city, there was a street performer named Marco who played the violin. Every day, he played beautiful music, hoping to save enough money to buy a new violin. One evening, a kind-hearted woman listened to his music and was moved. The next day, she returned with a surprise for Marco – a brand new violin. Overwhelmed with gratitude, Marco realized that his music had touched more lives than he had ever imagined.

1.21) What did Marco do in the city?

□ He wrote stories

□ He sold flowers

□ He painted pictures

□ He played the violin

1.22) What was Marco's hope while playing music?

□ To teach music

□ To travel the world

□ To become famous

□ To save money for a new violin

1.23) Who was moved by Marco's music?

□ A local shopkeeper

□ A young child

□ A kind-hearted woman

□ A group of tourists

1.24) What did the kind-hearted woman give to Marco?

☐ A bouquet of flowers

☐ A ticket to a concert

☐ A book of music

☐ A new violin

1.25) What did Marco realize after receiving the gift?

☐ He wanted to learn more instruments

☐ His music touched many lives

☐ He needed to practice more

☐ He should move to another city

Emily was an avid reader and dreamt of writing her own book one day. Each night, she would jot down ideas in her notebook. Her stories were filled with magical worlds and courageous characters. One day, her teacher noticed her passion for writing and encouraged her to enter a young writers' contest. Emily hesitated at first but then submitted her best story. To her surprise, she won the contest! This achievement filled her with confidence and fueled her dream to become an author.

1.26) What was Emily's dream?

☐ To become a scientist

☐ To be an actress

☐ To write her own book

☐ To travel the world

1.27) What did Emily do each night?

☐ Practiced playing piano

☐ Read a new book

☐ Jotted down ideas in a notebook

☐ Watched the stars

1.28) What kind of stories did Emily write?

☐ Magical worlds and courageous characters

☐ Historical events

☐ Real-life adventures

☐ Science fiction

1.29) Who encouraged Emily to enter a contest?

☐ A famous author

☐ Her parents

☐ Her best friend

☐ Her teacher

1.30) What was the outcome of the contest for Emily?

☐ She didn't win

☐ Her story was published

☐ She won the contest

☐ She came in second place

ALEXANDER-GRACE EDUCATION

Josh loved exploring the forest near his home, but one day he got lost. He wandered around, trying to find his way back. Suddenly, he saw a glowing path leading to a hidden cave. Inside the cave, he found a treasure chest filled with ancient artifacts. Josh decided to report his discovery to the local museum. His find turned out to be an important archaeological discovery, and Josh was hailed as a local hero for his honesty and adventurous spirit.

1.31) What did Josh love to do?

☐ Playing soccer

☐ Reading books

☐ Painting

☐ Exploring the forest

1.32) What happened to Josh in the forest?

☐ He found a rare animal

☐ He fell asleep

☐ He got lost

☐ He met a wizard

1.33) What did Josh find in the cave?

☐ A treasure chest with artifacts

☐ An ancient map

☐ A sleeping dragon

☐ A magic wand

1.34) What did Josh do with his discovery?

☐ Reported it to the museum

☐ Gave it to a friend

☐ Sold it

☐ Kept it for himself

1.35) How was Josh recognized for his actions?

☐ As a local hero

☐ As a talented musician

☐ As a skilled athlete

☐ As a great artist

Amelia had a big science test coming up and was nervous about it. She studied hard every day, but still felt unprepared. Her brother, who was good at science, offered to help her study. With his help, Amelia began to understand the concepts better. On the day of the test, she was confident and calm. After the test, she was thrilled to find out that she had scored the highest in her class. Amelia was grateful for her brother's help and realized the importance of asking for help when needed.

1.36) What was Amelia preparing for?

☐ A spelling bee

☐ A soccer match

☐ A science test

☐ A music recital

1.37) How did Amelia initially feel about the test?

☐ Nervous and unprepared

☐ Excited and confident

☐ Indifferent

☐ Overconfident

1.38) Who helped Amelia with her studies?

☐ Her mother

☐ Her best friend

☐ Her brother

☐ Her teacher

1.39) How did Amelia feel during the test?

☐ Confident and calm

☐ Rushed

☐ Scared and anxious

☐ Bored

1.40) What did Amelia learn from this experience?

☐ That science is easy

☐ That she is a genius

☐ The importance of asking for help

☐ That tests are unnecessary

Topic 1 – Answers

Question Number	Answer	Explanation
1.1	To chase a butterfly	Max followed a butterfly into Mr. Jenkins' garden.
1.2	Excited	Max loved exploring, indicating excitement.
1.3	A lonely old man	Max found Mr. Jenkins sitting alone.
1.4	Sad	Mr. Jenkins seemed sad before meeting Max.
1.5	Kindness can bring joy	Max's kindness brought joy to Mr. Jenkins.
1.6	A mural of her neighborhood	Lily decided to paint a mural of her neighborhood.
1.7	She loved her community	Lily's love for her community inspired her mural.
1.8	Proud	Lily felt proud while working on her mural.
1.9	They were impressed	Classmates were impressed by Lily's mural.
1.10	She can share her perspective through art	Lily learned she could express her view through art.
1.11	A hurt bird	Tommy found a hurt bird in his backyard.
1.12	He fed it and watched over it	Tommy cared for the bird by feeding and watching it.
1.13	It chirped happily	The bird chirped happily as it recovered.
1.14	Sad but understanding	Tommy was sad but understood it was right to free the bird.
1.15	Because it was well enough to fly	Tommy let the bird go because it could fly again.
1.16	Her grandmother	Sara enjoyed listening to her grandmother's stories.
1.17	A secret garden	Her grandmother told her about a secret garden.
1.18	Curiosity and love for adventure	Sara's curiosity and adventurous spirit led her to search.

1.19	A garden with colorful flowers and birds	Sara found a beautiful garden as described.
1.20	Stories can be real adventures	Sara learned stories could lead to real adventures.
1.21	He played the violin	Marco was a street performer who played the violin.
1.22	To save money for a new violin	Marco played music to save for a new violin.
1.23	A kind-hearted woman	A kind-hearted woman was moved by Marco's music.
1.24	A new violin	The woman gave Marco a new violin.
1.25	His music touched many lives	Marco realized his music impacted many people.
1.26	To write her own book	Emily dreamed of writing her own book.
1.27	Jotted down ideas in a notebook	Emily wrote ideas in her notebook each night.
1.28	Magical worlds and courageous characters	Emily's stories had magical and brave characters.
1.29	Her teacher	Emily's teacher encouraged her to enter a contest.
1.30	She won the contest	Emily won the young writers' contest.
1.31	Exploring the forest	Josh loved exploring the forest near his home.
1.32	He got lost	Josh got lost while exploring the forest.
1.33	A treasure chest with artifacts	Josh found a chest with ancient artifacts in the cave.
1.34	Reported it to the museum	Josh reported his discovery to the museum.
1.35	As a local hero	Josh was recognized as a hero for his honesty.
1.36	A science test	Amelia was preparing for a big science test.
1.37	Nervous and unprepared	Amelia felt nervous and unprepared for the test.
1.38	Her brother	Amelia's brother helped her study.
1.39	Confident and calm	Amelia felt confident and calm during the test.
1.40	The importance of asking for help	Amelia learned the value of seeking help.

Topic 2 – Identifying Literary Devices

2.1) What is a simile?

☐ Giving human qualities to non-human things

☐ A phrase with a hidden meaning

☐ A comparison using 'like' or 'as'

☐ Repeating the same sound at the beginning of words

2.2) Which of these is an example of alliteration?

☐ 'The wind whispered through the trees'

☐ 'She sells seashells by the seashore'

☐ 'As busy as a bee'

☐ 'My love is like a red, red rose'

2.3) What does an idiom mean?

☐ A comparison using 'like' or 'as'

☐ A word that sounds like its meaning

☐ A phrase with a meaning different from the literal meaning of its words

☐ A story with a moral

2.4) Find the metaphor: 'The classroom was a zoo.'

☐ The students were learning about zoos

☐ The classroom had pictures of animals

☐ There were many animals in the classroom

☐ The classroom was very noisy and chaotic

2.5) What is alliteration?

☐ Using words that imitate sounds

☐ Repeating the first consonant sounds in words

☐ Giving human qualities to non-human things

☐ A comparison using 'like' or 'as'

2.6) Choose the sentence with onomatopoeia.

☐ 'The bees buzzed in the garden'

☐ 'The flowers in the garden were very tall'

☐ 'The garden was as lovely as a painting'

☐ 'The garden was silent'

2.7) What is personification?

☐ An exaggeration for effect

☐ A comparison not using 'like' or 'as'

☐ Giving human qualities to non-human things

☐ A phrase with a different meaning from its literal words

2.8) Which of these is an example of a metaphor?

☐ 'The alarm clock screamed in the morning'

☐ 'Busy as a bee'

☐ 'The wind flew through the trees'

☐ 'Time is a thief'

2.9) Find the hyperbole: 'I am so hungry I could eat a horse.'

☐ Actually eating a horse

☐ Preferring to eat horse meat

☐ Being a little bit hungry

☐ Exaggerating about being very hungry

2.10) What does 'It's raining cats and dogs' mean?

☐ There are many animals outside

☐ Cats and dogs are falling from the sky

☐ It's raining very heavily

☐ It's a sunny day

2.11) Which sentence uses a simile?

☐ 'The moon is a glowing ball in the sky'

☐ 'The cat was as quiet as a mouse'

☐ 'Her smile was sunshine'

☐ 'The car roared down the street'

2.12) What does the idiom 'piece of cake' mean?

☐ Something very easy to do

☐ A difficult task

☐ A delicious dessert

☐ A small piece of a cake

2.13) Which of these is an example of personification?

☐ 'The stars danced in the sky'

☐ 'The wind went through the trees'

☐ 'She is as fast as a cheetah'

☐ 'He swims like a fish'

2.14) Find the hyperbole: 'Her smile could light up a room.'

☐ She is holding a flashlight

☐ The room is very dark

☐ Her smile actually producing light

☐ Exaggerating about how bright her smile is

2.15) What is an idiom?

☐ A phrase whose meaning is different from the literal meaning of the words

☐ Exaggeration for dramatic effect

☐ A comparison using 'like' or 'as'

☐ Repeating the same sound at the beginning of words

2.16) Choose the sentence with a metaphor stating that there are ups and downs.

☐ 'Life is a rollercoaster'

☐ 'The car is as fast as a rocket'

☐ 'The stars are sparkling diamonds'

☐ 'The thunder roared like a lion'

2.17) What does 'break a leg' mean in theater?

☐ Perform poorly

☐ Stop the performance

☐ Actually breaking a leg

☐ Good luck

2.18) Which of these is an example of alliteration?

☐ 'Slippery snakes slide silently'

☐ 'The dog barked loudly'

☐ 'The flowers are blooming'

☐ 'The sun is very bright'

2.19) What does the idiom 'out of the blue' mean?

☐ Something unexpected

☐ The color blue

☐ A clear sky

☐ Feeling sad

2.20) What does the following simile mean: 'He runs like the wind.'

☐ He doesn't like running

☐ He can control the wind

☐ He runs during windy weather

☐ Comparing his running speed to the wind

ALEXANDER-GRACE EDUCATION

2.21) What does the idiom 'a piece of cake' mean?

☐ A delicious dessert

☐ Something that is very easy to do

☐ A complicated task

☐ A part of a cake

2.22) Choose the sentence that is an example of hyperbole:

☐ 'The cat sleeps all day'

☐ 'I have a million things to do today'

☐ 'The book was interesting'

☐ 'The flowers are blooming'

2.23) What is a metaphor?

☐ An exaggeration for dramatic effect

☐ A direct comparison between two things without using 'like' or 'as'

☐ Giving human qualities to non-human things

☐ A comparison using 'like' or 'as'

2.24) Which of these is an example of onomatopoeia?

☐ 'The leaves fell gently to the ground'

☐ 'The sun shone brightly'

☐ 'The bees buzzed in the garden'

☐ 'The stars twinkled in the night sky'

2.25) What does the personification 'the sun smiled down on us' mean?

☐ The sun is actually smiling

☐ It was a sunny day

☐ People were smiling in the sunlight

☐ Giving the sun the human quality of smiling

2.26) What is alliteration?

☐ Comparing two things using 'like' or 'as'

☐ Using words that sound like their meaning

☐ Repeating the same beginning sound in adjacent or closely connected words

☐ A phrase that means something different than what it says

2.27) What does the idiom 'hit the books' mean?

☐ To start studying

☐ To physically hit books

☐ To read a book quickly

☐ To write a book

2.28) Which of these is a simile?

☐ 'He is a shining star'

☐ 'The classroom was a zoo'

☐ 'She is as brave as a lion'

☐ 'The thunder roared'

2.29) Explain the metaphor: 'Time is a thief.'

☐ Time actually stealing things

☐ Being robbed of time

☐ Time moving quickly

☐ Comparing time to a thief without using 'like' or 'as'

2.30) What does the idiom 'when pigs fly' mean?

☐ Something that will never happen

☐ A story about pigs

☐ Pigs actually flying

☐ A very likely event

2.31) Which sentence is an example of a metaphor?

☐ 'He swims like a fish'

☐ 'She is as fast as a cheetah'

☐ 'Life is a journey'

☐ 'The car beeped loudly'

2.32) What does the idiom 'under the weather' mean?

☐ Being outside in bad weather

☐ Understanding weather patterns

☐ Hiding something

☐ Feeling ill or not well

2.33) Choose the sentence that uses onomatopoeia:

☐ 'The stars are twinkling in the sky'

☐ 'The clock ticked loudly as he worked'

☐ 'She was as graceful as a swan'

☐ 'The moon was a ghostly galleon'

2.34) Explain the simile: 'Her eyes sparkled like diamonds.'

☐ Comparing her eyes to diamonds with 'like'

☐ Her eyes can cut like diamonds

☐ Her eyes were actually made of diamonds

☐ She was wearing diamond earrings

2.35) What is an idiom?

☐ A direct comparison using 'like' or 'as'

☐ Repeating the first consonant sounds in words

☐ An exaggeration for dramatic effect

☐ A phrase where the meaning is not literal or direct

2.36) Which of these is an example of hyperbole?

☐ 'The car is as fast as a cheetah'

☐ 'The cat sleeps all day'

☐ 'I'm so hungry I could eat a horse'

☐ 'The book was interesting'

ALEXANDER-GRACE EDUCATION

2.37) What does the idiom 'cold feet' mean?

□ To be calm and relaxed

□ To walk on cold surfaces

□ To have actually cold feet

□ To be nervous or hesitant

2.38) Choose the sentence with alliteration:

□ 'The sun glowed brightly in the sky'

□ 'Silly Sally swiftly shooed seven silly sheep'

□ 'The cat is calm and cool'

□ 'He runs quickly around the room'

2.39) Explain the example of personification: 'The leaves danced in the wind.'

□ The leaves are actually dancing

□ People were dancing with leaves

□ Giving the leaves the human action of dancing

□ The wind was very strong

2.40) What does the idiom 'hit the nail on the head' mean?

□ To start building something

□ To do or say something exactly right

□ To make a mistake

□ To actually hit a nail with a hammer

Topic 2 - Answers

Question Number	Answer	Explanation
2.1	A comparison using 'like' or 'as'	Simile is a figure of speech comparing two things using 'like' or 'as'.
2.2	'She sells seashells by the seashore'	Alliteration is the repetition of the same sound at the beginning of adjacent words.
2.3	A phrase with a meaning different from the literal meaning of its words	An idiom is a phrase where the meaning isn't obvious from the individual words.
2.4	The classroom was very noisy and chaotic	A metaphor makes a direct comparison, saying one thing is another.
2.5	Repeating the first consonant sounds in words	Alliteration is the repetition of the same initial consonant sound in adjacent or closely connected words.
2.6	'The bees buzzed in the garden'	Onomatopoeia is the use of words that imitate sounds.
2.7	Giving human qualities to non-human things	Personification is attributing human characteristics to non-human entities.
2.8	'Time is a thief'	A metaphor is a figure of speech that makes a direct comparison without using 'like' or 'as'.
2.9	Exaggerating about being very hungry	Hyperbole is an exaggeration used for emphasis or humor.
2.10	It's raining very heavily	This idiom means it is raining a lot, not literally cats and dogs.
2.11	'The cat was as quiet as a mouse'	A simile uses 'like' or 'as' to make a comparison.
2.12	Something very easy to do	The idiom 'piece of cake' means something is very easy.
2.13	'The stars danced in the sky'	Personification is giving human qualities to non-human things.
2.14	Exaggerating about how bright her smile is	Hyperbole is an exaggeration for effect, not meant to be taken literally.
2.15	A phrase whose meaning is different from the literal meaning of the words	An idiom is a common phrase or expression with a meaning different from its literal interpretation.
2.16	'Life is a rollercoaster'	A metaphor is a figure of speech that says one thing is another.
2.17	Good luck	In theater, 'break a leg' is an idiom used to wish performers good luck.
2.18	'Slippery snakes slide silently'	Alliteration involves the repetition of the same initial sound in successive words.
2.19	Something unexpected	'Out of the blue' means something happens unexpectedly.

2.20	Comparing his running speed to the wind	A simile compares two things using 'like' or 'as'.
2.21	Something that is very easy to do	The idiom 'a piece of cake' means something is easy to accomplish.
2.22	'I have a million things to do today'	Hyperbole is an exaggerated statement not meant to be taken literally.
2.23	A direct comparison between two things without using 'like' or 'as'	A metaphor directly compares two things without 'like' or 'as'.
2.24	'The bees buzzed in the garden'	Onomatopoeia uses words that mimic the sounds they describe.
2.25	Giving the sun the human quality of smiling	Personification attributes human characteristics to non-human things.
2.26	Repeating the same beginning sound in adjacent or closely connected words	Alliteration is the repetition of initial consonant sounds in neighboring words.
2.27	To start studying	'Hit the books' is an idiom meaning to begin studying.
2.28	'She is as brave as a lion'	A simile uses 'like' or 'as' to make comparisons.
2.29	Comparing time to a thief without using 'like' or 'as'	A metaphor makes a direct comparison without using 'like' or 'as'.
2.30	Something that will never happen	'When pigs fly' is an idiom used to describe something that is very unlikely to happen.
2.31	'Life is a journey'	A metaphor directly compares life to a journey.
2.32	Feeling ill or not well	'Under the weather' is an idiom meaning feeling sick or unwell.
2.33	'The clock ticked loudly as he worked'	Onomatopoeia involves words that sound like the thing they describe.
2.34	Comparing her eyes to diamonds with 'like'	A simile uses 'like' or 'as' to compare two things.
2.35	A phrase where the meaning is not literal or direct	An idiom is a phrase that means something different than its literal meaning.
2.36	'I'm so hungry I could eat a horse'	Hyperbole is an exaggerated statement for dramatic effect.
2.37	To be nervous or hesitant	'Cold feet' is an idiom that means feeling nervous or hesitant.
2.38	'Silly Sally swiftly shooed seven silly sheep'	Alliteration is the repetition of the same beginning sounds in a series of words.
2.39	Giving the leaves the human action of dancing	Personification gives human characteristics to non-human things.
2.40	To do or say something exactly right	'Hit the nail on the head' means to do or say something that is exactly right.

Topic 3 - Definitions

3.1) What is an 'environment'?

☐ A type of building.

☐ The surroundings where we live.

☐ A subject in school.

☐ A place in a story.

3.2) What does 'respect' mean?

☐ Learning a new skill.

☐ Admiring someone for their abilities or qualities.

☐ Playing a game fairly.

☐ Sharing things with friends.

3.3) Define 'community'.

☐ Different types of plants.

☐ A collection of books.

☐ A group of students in a class.

☐ People living together in one place.

3.4) What is a 'responsibility'?

☐ A holiday celebration.

☐ A duty or task you are expected to do.

☐ A type of weather.

☐ A game played in teams.

3.5) Define 'cooperation'.

☐ Drawing a picture.

☐ Playing a solo game.

☐ Reading a book.

☐ Working together with others.

3.6) What does 'courage' mean?

☐ Learning a new language.

☐ Being brave when facing difficulties.

☐ Helping someone in need.

☐ Remembering something important.

3.7) Define 'honesty'.

☐ Drawing a picture accurately.

☐ Playing a musical instrument.

☐ Always telling the truth.

☐ Sharing your things.

3.8) What is 'patience'?

☐ Solving a math problem.

☐ Reading a long book.

☐ Waiting calmly for something.

☐ Running fast in a race.

3.9) Define 'curiosity'.

☐ Wanting to learn about something.

☐ Drawing a new picture.

☐ Playing a new sport.

☐ Making a new friend.

3.10) What does 'imagination' mean?

☐ Learning how to cook.

☐ Creating ideas in your mind.

☐ Playing a board game.

☐ Remembering past events.

3.11) What is 'creativity'?

☐ A subject in school.

☐ Using imagination to create something.

☐ A type of animal.

☐ Playing a sport.

3.12) Define 'wisdom'.

☐ Having knowledge and good judgment.

☐ A type of tree.

☐ A kind of bird.

☐ A holiday.

3.13) What does 'energy' mean?

☐ A subject in school.

☐ A kind of car.

☐ A type of drink.

☐ The strength required for physical or mental activity.

3.14) Define 'friendship'.

☐ A close relationship between people.

☐ A book about adventures.

☐ A game played together.

☐ A type of food.

3.15) What is 'compassion'?

☐ A computer program.

☐ Caring deeply about others' feelings.

☐ A musical instrument.

☐ A type of exercise.

3.16) Define 'curiosity'.

☐ A type of game.

☐ A kind of dance.

☐ Eager to know or learn something.

☐ A school subject.

3.17) What does 'bravery' mean?

☐ Being courageous and facing fears.

☐ A school event.

☐ A computer game.

☐ A type of clothing.

3.18) Define 'adventure'.

☐ A kind of vehicle.

☐ A type of fruit.

☐ An exciting or unusual experience.

☐ A school subject.

3.19) What is 'knowledge'?

☐ Information, understanding, or skill gained by experience.

☐ A piece of furniture.

☐ A kind of animal.

☐ A type of food.

3.20) Define 'laughter'.

☐ A school activity.

☐ A musical note.

☐ The action or sound of laughing.

☐ A type of book.

3.21) What does 'gratitude' mean?

☐ Playing a game.

☐ A type of music.

☐ Feeling thankful and appreciative.

☐ A kind of bird.

3.22) Define 'adventure'.

☐ An exciting and unusual experience.

☐ A school project.

☐ A kind of tool.

☐ A type of food.

3.23) What is 'generosity'?

☐ A school subject.

☐ A kind of animal.

☐ Willingness to give and share freely.

☐ A type of game.

3.24) Define 'perseverance'.

☐ A musical instrument.

☐ A holiday.

☐ Continuing to do something despite difficulties.

☐ A type of dance.

3.25) What does 'curiosity' mean?

□ A kind of plant.

□ A type of clothing.

□ A part of a car.

□ Eager to learn or know something.

3.26) Define 'empathy'.

□ A kind of food.

□ Understanding and sharing the feelings of another.

□ A school event.

□ A sport.

3.27) What is 'optimism'?

□ A type of weather.

□ Playing a sport.

□ A kind of animal.

□ Hopefulness and confidence about the future.

3.28) Define 'integrity'.

□ A computer program.

□ A type of game.

□ The quality of being honest and having strong moral principles.

□ A musical genre.

3.29) What does 'humor' mean?

☐ A school subject.

☐ A type of plant.

☐ A piece of furniture.

☐ The quality of being amusing or comic.

3.30) Define 'confidence'.

☐ A type of animal.

☐ A kind of tool.

☐ The feeling of self-assurance arising from one's abilities or qualities.

☐ A school project.

3.31) What is 'innovation'?

☐ A type of animal.

☐ A school game.

☐ A musical instrument.

☐ Creating new ideas or methods.

3.32) Define 'loyalty'.

☐ Playing a sport.

☐ A school subject.

☐ Being faithful to someone or something.

☐ A type of food.

3.33) What does 'courage' mean?

☐ Being brave and facing challenges.

☐ A school event.

☐ A type of dance.

☐ A kind of tree.

3.34) Define 'harmony'.

☐ A musical note.

☐ Living or working together in a peaceful way.

☐ A game.

☐ A type of food.

3.35) What is 'justice'?

☐ A kind of animal.

☐ Fairness in the way people are treated.

☐ A type of plant.

☐ A holiday.

3.36) Define 'determination'.

☐ Not giving up, even when things are tough.

☐ A kind of bird.

☐ A school project.

☐ A type of car.

3.37) What does 'freedom' mean?

□ A sport.

□ A school subject.

□ A type of clothing.

□ Having the right to act, speak, or think as one wants.

3.38) Define 'wisdom'.

□ A holiday.

□ A musical instrument.

□ A kind of tool.

□ Having knowledge and good judgment.

3.39) What is 'compassion'?

□ A kind of food.

□ A school event.

□ A type of game.

□ Caring deeply about others' feelings.

3.40) Define 'teamwork'.

□ A piece of furniture.

□ Working together with others to achieve a goal.

□ A school activity.

□ A type of book.

Topic 3 - Answers

Question Number	Answer	Explanation
3.1	The surroundings where we live.	'Environment' refers to the natural or man-made surroundings.
3.2	Admiring someone for their abilities or qualities.	'Respect' means showing admiration for someone's abilities or qualities.
3.3	People living together in one place.	'Community' refers to a group of people living in the same place.
3.4	A duty or task you are expected to do.	'Responsibility' involves a duty or task one should perform.
3.5	Working together with others.	'Cooperation' is the act of working together towards a common goal.
3.6	Being brave when facing difficulties.	'Courage' means showing bravery in challenging situations.
3.7	Always telling the truth.	'Honesty' is the quality of being truthful and sincere.
3.8	Waiting calmly for something.	'Patience' is the ability to wait for something without frustration.
3.9	Wanting to learn about something.	'Curiosity' is the desire to learn or know about something.
3.10	Creating ideas in your mind.	'Imagination' involves forming new ideas or images in the mind.
3.11	Using imagination to create something.	'Creativity' is the use of imagination to produce new ideas.
3.12	Having knowledge and good judgment.	'Wisdom' involves having experience, knowledge, and good judgment.
3.13	The strength required for physical or mental activity.	'Energy' is the capacity to do work or perform activities.
3.14	A close relationship between people.	'Friendship' is a bond of mutual affection between people.
3.15	Caring deeply about others' feelings.	'Compassion' is showing sympathy and concern for others.
3.16	Eager to know or learn something.	'Curiosity' is a strong desire to know or learn about something.
3.17	Being courageous and facing fears.	'Bravery' is showing courage and not being afraid in difficult situations.
3.18	An exciting or unusual experience.	'Adventure' involves engaging in exciting or unusual experiences.

3.19	Information, understanding, or skill gained by experience.	'Knowledge' refers to what is known in a particular field or in total.
3.20	The action or sound of laughing.	'Laughter' is the act or sound of laughing.
3.21	Feeling thankful and appreciative.	'Gratitude' is showing thankfulness and appreciation.
3.22	An exciting and unusual experience.	'Adventure' is an experience that is thrilling and unusual.
3.23	Willingness to give and share freely.	'Generosity' is the quality of being willing to share with others.
3.24	Continuing to do something despite difficulties.	'Perseverance' is the persistence in doing something despite challenges.
3.25	Eager to learn or know something.	'Curiosity' is the desire to learn more about something.
3.26	Understanding and sharing the feelings of another.	'Empathy' is the ability to understand and share someone's feelings.
3.27	Hopefulness and confidence about the future.	'Optimism' is having a positive outlook on the future.
3.28	The quality of being honest and having strong moral principles.	'Integrity' involves being honest and upholding strong moral principles.
3.29	The quality of being amusing or comic.	'Humor' is the ability to be funny or amusing.
3.30	The feeling of self-assurance arising from one's abilities or qualities.	'Confidence' is feeling sure about one's abilities or qualities.
3.31	Creating new ideas or methods.	'Innovation' involves coming up with new ideas or methods.
3.32	Being faithful to someone or something.	'Loyalty' is showing faithfulness or devotion to someone or something.
3.33	Being brave and facing challenges.	'Courage' is the quality of being brave in facing challenges.
3.34	Living or working together in a peaceful way.	'Harmony' is a state of peaceful existence and cooperation.
3.35	Fairness in the way people are treated.	'Justice' involves fairness and moral righteousness.
3.36	Not giving up, even when things are tough.	'Determination' is the firmness of purpose and not giving up.
3.37	Having the right to act, speak, or think as one wants.	'Freedom' is the state of being free to express oneself.
3.38	Having knowledge and good judgment.	'Wisdom' is possessing knowledge, experience, and sound judgment.
3.39	Caring deeply about others' feelings.	'Compassion' is showing deep sympathy and concern for others.
3.40	Working together with others to achieve a goal.	'Teamwork' is the collaborative effort of a group to achieve a common goal.

Topic 4 – Exploring Figurative Language

One sunny day, the sky was as blue as an ocean, and the flowers danced in the wind. Tommy, a brave as a lion boy, decided to go on an adventure. He walked through the forest, which was a sea of green, and talked to the birds that sang songs sweeter than honey. As the day turned into night, the stars twinkled like diamonds in the sky. Tommy returned home, happy as a clam, with stories that were music to his mother's ears.

4.1) In the story, what does 'the sky was as blue as an ocean' mean?

□ The sky was filled with fish.

□ The sky had waves.

□ The sky was very blue.

□ The sky was wet.

4.2) What does 'flowers danced in the wind' suggest?

□ The flowers were moving gently.

□ The flowers were tired.

□ The flowers were actually dancing.

□ The flowers were playing music.

4.3) How is Tommy described?

□ As quiet as a mouse.

□ As funny as a clown.

□ As fast as a cheetah.

□ As brave as a lion.

4.4) What does 'a sea of green' tell us about the forest?

☐ The forest had fish in it.

☐ The forest was filled with water.

☐ The forest was very green.

☐ The forest was a large body of water.

4.5) What is meant by 'stars twinkled like diamonds'?

☐ The stars were shining brightly.

☐ The stars were singing.

☐ The stars were expensive.

☐ The stars were made of diamonds.

In a small village, there was a house where laughter never ended. Sarah, who had a heart of gold, lived there with her family. One evening, the moon shone like a silver coin, and Sarah decided to explore the garden. She found flowers whispering secrets and trees standing like silent guardians. When she returned, her grandmother's stories took them on a magic carpet ride to distant lands.

4.6) What does 'a house where laughter never ended' suggest?

☐ The house was playing music.

☐ The house was always happy.

☐ The house was very loud.

☐ The house was very big.

4.7) How is Sarah described?

☐ Having eyes like a hawk.

☐ Having a mind like a computer.

☐ Having a heart of gold.

☐ Having feet like wings.

4.8) What is meant by 'moon shone like a silver coin'?

☐ The moon was round like a coin.

☐ The moon was very bright.

☐ The moon was valuable.

☐ The moon was made of silver.

4.9) What does 'flowers whispering secrets' mean?

☐ The flowers knew something unknown.

☐ The flowers seemed to be talking softly.

☐ The flowers were very quiet.

☐ The flowers were keeping secrets.

4.10) How does the phrase 'magic carpet ride' work in the story?

☐ It describes an imaginative journey.

☐ It means they had a carpet that could fly.

☐ It means they went on a trip.

☐ It suggests they were cleaning the carpet.

Max, a young detective with eyes like a hawk, was on a mission. He moved through the city streets, quiet as a shadow. The night was as black as ink, but Max's determination was as solid as a rock. He solved the mystery just as the dawn painted the sky with strokes of pink and orange.

4.11) What does 'eyes like a hawk' suggest about Max?

☐ He liked to hunt.

☐ He could fly.

☐ He had feathers.

☐ He was very observant.

4.12) What is meant by 'quiet as a shadow'?

☐ Feeling scared.

☐ Being very dark.

☐ Moving silently.

☐ Staying still.

4.13) How does 'night was as black as ink' describe the setting?

☐ Very dark night.

☐ A scary night.

☐ A night with many stars.

☐ A night full of writing.

4.14) What does 'determination was as solid as a rock' tell us about Max?

□ He was very determined.

□ He was standing on a rock.

□ He was unmovable.

□ He was strong like a rock.

4.15) What does 'dawn painted the sky' mean?

□ The sky had a picture on it.

□ The sky changed colors at sunrise.

□ Someone was painting the sky.

□ The sky was being cleaned.

In a magical forest, a river ran like a ribbon of glass. Ellie, curious as a cat, followed its path. She found trees that whispered ancient tales and flowers that sang with the voices of angels. As the sun set, painting the sky in shades of purple and gold, Ellie's heart swelled with joy.

4.16) What does 'sweeter than honey' suggest about the pies?

□ The pies attracted bees.

□ The pies had honey in them.

□ The pies were very sweet.

□ The pies were sticky.

4.17) How is the traveler described?

□ With a voice as loud as thunder.

□ With eyes as bright as stars.

□ With hair like the night sky.

□ With a smile like the sun.

4.18) What is meant by 'laughter like a melody'?

☐ The laughter was a song.

☐ The laughter was annoying.

☐ The laughter was pleasant to hear.

☐ The laughter was very loud.

4.19) How does 'painted the sky in shades of orange and pink' work in the story?

☐ It means someone was painting the sky.

☐ It suggests the sky was colorful.

☐ It describes a beautiful sunset.

☐ It indicates the sky was changing.

4.20) What does 'as if an artist had brushed colors' mean?

☐ There was an artist in the sky.

☐ The sky looked like a painting.

☐ The sky was a canvas.

☐ The sky had many colors.

On top of a snowy hill, there was a cabin that glowed like a beacon of warmth. Inside, Emily, gentle as a dove, was knitting a scarf as long as a snake. Outside, the snowflakes were like a blanket of white, and the trees stood like silent giants. The fireplace crackled like a chorus of crickets, making the cabin cozy on the chilly night.

4.16) What does 'glowed like a beacon of warmth' suggest about the cabin?

☐ The cabin had a lighthouse.

☐ The cabin had a bright light.

☐ The cabin was on fire.

☐ The cabin was very warm and inviting.

4.17) How is Emily described?

☐ Proud as a peacock.

☐ Busy as a bee.

☐ Gentle as a dove.

☐ Happy as a clam.

4.18) What is meant by 'snowflakes were like a blanket of white'?

☐ The snow was heavy like a blanket.

☐ The snow was colorful.

☐ The snow covered everything softly.

☐ The snow was used to make a blanket.

4.19) How does 'the fireplace crackled like a chorus of crickets' work in the story?

☐ It implies the fireplace was singing.

☐ It suggests the fireplace made a soft, pleasant sound.

☐ It means the fireplace was filled with crickets.

☐ It indicates the fireplace was very loud.

4.20) What does 'stood like silent giants' mean?

☐ The trees were scared.

☐ The trees were making a lot of noise.

☐ The trees were moving.

☐ The trees were very tall and quiet.

In a magical forest, there was a tree as old as time itself. Beneath its branches, Lily, light as a feather, danced with the fireflies that sparkled like tiny stars. The brook nearby babbled like it was telling a story, and the leaves rustled as if sharing secrets. As the moon climbed high, shining like a silver lantern, Lily felt as if she was part of a fairy tale.

4.21) What does 'a tree as old as time itself' suggest?

☐ The tree was young.

☐ The tree was very old.

☐ The tree had a clock in it.

☐ The tree was telling time.

4.22) How is Lily described?

☐ Strong as an ox.

☐ Bright as the sun.

☐ Quiet as a mouse.

☐ Light as a feather.

4.23) What is meant by 'fireflies that sparkled like tiny stars'?

☐ The fireflies were not visible.

☐ The fireflies were shining brightly.

☐ The fireflies were up in the sky.

☐ The fireflies were actual stars.

4.24) How does 'the brook babbled like it was telling a story' work in the story?

☐ It implies the brook had a mouth.

☐ It means the brook was reading a book.

☐ It suggests the brook made a continuous sound.

☐ It indicates the brook was silent.

4.25) What does 'leaves rustled as if sharing secrets' mean?

☐ The leaves were keeping secrets.

☐ The leaves were silent.

☐ The leaves were making soft noises.

☐ The leaves were whispering.

In a mystical forest, there was a crystal-clear lake that mirrored the sky. Alice, gentle as a summer breeze, wandered near the lake, where the leaves rustled like a symphony of nature. The flowers around the lake glowed like tiny suns, and the frogs croaked as if they were telling old tales. As night fell, the fireflies danced around Alice, turning the forest into a wonderland of lights.

4.26) What does 'a crystal-clear lake that mirrored the sky' suggest?

☐ The lake was very clear and reflective.

☐ The lake had a mirror in it.

☐ The lake was as high as the sky.

☐ The lake was made of crystal.

4.27) How is Alice described?

☐ Gentle as a summer breeze.

☐ Quick as a rabbit.

☐ Bright as the sun.

☐ Quiet as a mouse.

4.28) What is meant by 'leaves rustled like a symphony of nature'?

☐ The leaves were playing instruments.

☐ The leaves were singing.

☐ The sound of leaves was pleasant and musical.

☐ The leaves were very noisy.

4.29) How does 'fireflies danced around Alice' work in the story?

☐ It means the fireflies were dancing with Alice.

☐ It suggests the fireflies were moving playfully.

☐ It indicates the fireflies were on fire.

☐ It implies the fireflies were playing music.

4.30) What does 'turning the forest into a wonderland of lights' mean?

☐ Turning the forest into an amusement park.

☐ Decorating the forest with light bulbs.

☐ Making the forest look magical with lights.

☐ Lighting up the forest with lamps.

In a vibrant town, there was a market that buzzed like a hive of bees. Sam, quick-witted as a fox, wandered through the stalls, where the scents of spices hung in the air like a warm embrace. The fabrics on display were a rainbow of colors, and the chatter of the crowd was like a melody. As Sam explored, the market seemed like a tapestry of tales and treasures.

4.31) What does 'buzzed like a hive of bees' suggest about the market?

☐ The market was lively and busy.

☐ The market was selling honey.

☐ The market was making buzzing sounds.

☐ The market had many bees.

4.32) How is Sam described?

☐ Strong as an ox.

☐ Loud as a lion.

☐ Graceful as a swan.

☐ Quick-witted as a fox.

4.33) What is meant by 'scents of spices hung in the air like a warm embrace'?

☐ The air was filled with comforting smells.

☐ The spices were floating in the air.

☐ The air was hot and spicy.

☐ The spices were hugging people.

4.34) How does 'fabrics on display were a rainbow of colors' work in the story?

☐ The fabrics were very colorful.

☐ The fabrics were in the sky.

☐ The fabrics were creating a rainbow.

☐ The fabrics were wet from rain.

4.35) What does 'tapestry of tales and treasures' mean?

☐ The market was selling tapestries.

☐ The market had a treasure hunt.

☐ The market was telling a story.

☐ The market was full of interesting stories and items.

At the edge of a quiet village, there was a garden where time seemed to stand still. Lily, curious as a cat, explored the garden, marveling at the dewdrops that sparkled like tiny stars on the petals. The hummingbirds fluttered like tiny dancers, and the fragrance of the flowers was a symphony to the senses. In this garden, every moment felt like a page from a fairy tale.

4.36) What does 'time seemed to stand still' suggest about the garden?

□ The garden was frozen.

□ The garden was peaceful and calm.

□ The garden was old.

□ The garden had a clock that stopped.

4.37) How is Lily described?

□ Curious as a cat.

□ Brave as a lion.

□ Busy as a bee.

□ Quiet as a mouse.

4.38) What is meant by 'dewdrops sparkled like tiny stars'?

□ The dewdrops were in the sky.

□ The dewdrops were shining brightly.

□ The dewdrops were like real stars.

□ The dewdrops were very large.

4.39) How does 'hummingbirds fluttered like tiny dancers' work in the story?

□ The hummingbirds were on a stage.

□ The hummingbirds were wearing costumes.

□ The hummingbirds were dancing.

□ The hummingbirds moved gracefully.

4.40) What does 'every moment felt like a page from a fairy tale' mean?

☐ There were books in the garden.

☐ The garden told a story.

☐ The garden experience was magical and special.

☐ The garden was unreal.

Topic 4 - Answers

Question Number	Answer	Explanation
4.1	The sky was very blue.	This simile compares the color of the sky to the deep blue of an ocean.
4.2	The flowers were moving gently.	This phrase suggests that the flowers were swaying in the wind.
4.3	As brave as a lion.	Tommy is described as being very brave, like a lion.
4.4	The forest was very green.	"A sea of green" implies that the forest was lush and densely green.
4.5	The stars were shining brightly.	This simile compares the sparkling of stars to the shine of diamoncs.
4.6	The house was always happy.	This phrase suggests constant happiness in the house.
4.7	Having a heart of gold.	Sarah is described as being very kind and caring.
4.8	The moon was very bright.	This simile compares the brightness of the moon to a shiny silver coin.
4.9	The flowers seemed to be talking softly.	This phrase personifies the flowers as if they were whispering secrets.
4.10	It describes an imaginative journey.	"Magic carpet ride" is used to describe a journey of imagination.
4.11	He was very observant.	"Eyes like a hawk" suggests that Max was very observant and alert.
4.12	Moving silently.	Being "quiet as a shadow" means moving silently and stealthily.
4.13	Very dark night.	"Night was as black as ink" describes the darkness of the night.
4.14	He was very determined.	This metaphor suggests that Max's determination was unshakeable.
4.15	The sky changed colors at sunrise.	"Dawn painted the sky" means the sky was changing colors at sunrise.
4.16	The lake was very clear and reflective.	Describes the clarity and reflective quality of the lake.
4.17	Gentle as a summer breeze.	Alice is described as being gentle and soft.
4.18	The sound of leaves was pleasant and musical.	"Leaves rustled like a symphony" suggests a harmonious sound.

4.19	It suggests the fireflies were moving playfully.	"Fireflies danced around Alice" implies a playful, light movement.
4.20	Making the forest look magical with lights.	The phrase suggests a magical, illuminated forest atmosphere.
4.21	The tree was very old.	Suggests the ancient age of the tree, like the concept of time.
4.22	Light as a feather.	Lily is described as being light and graceful.
4.23	The fireflies were shining brightly.	Compares the glow of fireflies to the brightness of stars.
4.24	It suggests the brook made a continuous sound.	"The brook babbled" personifies the sound of the flowing water.
4.25	The leaves were making soft noises.	Suggests the leaves were rustling softly, like sharing secrets.
4.26	The cabin was very warm and inviting.	The phrase implies the cabin was a welcoming, warm place.
4.27	Gentle as a summer breeze.	Describes Alice as being gentle and soothing.
4.28	The sound of leaves was pleasant and musical.	Suggests the leaves created a harmonious, pleasant sound.
4.29	It suggests the fireflies were moving playfully.	Implies the fireflies were moving around Alice in a playful manner.
4.30	Making the forest look magical with lights.	Describes a magical appearance of the forest with glowing fireflies.
4.31	The market was lively and busy.	Indicates a bustling, active environment in the market.
4.32	Quick-witted as a fox.	Describes Sam as being smart and clever.
4.33	The air was filled with comforting smells.	Indicates that the air was rich with the pleasant aromas of spices.
4.34	The fabrics were very colorful.	Describes a wide range of colors in the fabrics on display.
4.35	The market was full of interesting stories and items.	Suggests a variety of intriguing finds and experiences at the market.
4.36	The garden was peaceful and calm.	Implies a tranquil, timeless atmosphere in the garden.
4.37	Curious as a cat.	Lily is described as being inquisitive and interested.
4.38	The dewdrops were shining brightly.	Suggests that the dewdrops glistened like small stars.
4.39	The hummingbirds moved gracefully.	Implies the delicate and elegant movement of hummingbirds.
4.40	The garden experience was magical and special.	Suggests the garden had a fairy-tale-like, enchanting quality.

Topic 5 – Recognizing Author's Craft

In the quaint village of Maplewood, nestled among lush forests and sparkling streams, lived a young girl named Emily. Emily loved exploring the woods, where she often imagined herself as a brave adventurer. One sunny afternoon, while wandering through the forest, Emily stumbled upon an ancient, moss-covered stone well. She had never seen it before. Curiosity piqued, she peered into the well, only to find an old, leather-bound book lying at the bottom. With effort, she retrieved the book and opened it to discover it was a diary belonging to her great-grandmother, filled with stories of hidden treasures and magical creatures in Maplewood. Each page she turned unraveled secrets and adventures of the past, making her see her familiar village in a whole new light.

5.1) What element of foreshadowing can be seen in Emily finding the ancient well?

☐ A lesson in geography

☐ A new friend at school that she once thought didn't like her

☐ A return to her home which she loved

☐ An upcoming adventure of family discovery

5.2) How does the author create a sense of mystery in the story?

☐ By describing Emily's daily routine

☐ By focusing on Emily's school life

☐ Through the sudden discovery of the well and the diary

☐ By introducing a talking animal

5.3) The diary belonging to Emily's great-grandmother primarily adds which element to the story?

☐ Comic relief

☐ Modern technology

☐ Historical depth and magical allure

☐ Everyday realism

5.4) How does the setting of Maplewood contribute to the narrative?

☐ It emphasizes the importance of education

☐ It serves as a contrast to city life

☐ It offers a backdrop for technological advancements

☐ It provides a mystical and adventurous atmosphere

5.5) The author's tone in narrating Emily's discovery can best be described as:

☐ Straightforward and factual

☐ Sarcastic and humorous

☐ Formal and informative

☐ Mysterious and engaging

In the bustling city of Newhaven, a clever boy named Alex discovered a mysterious old compass in his grandfather's attic. The compass, unlike any other, pointed to locations that didn't exist on any map. Fascinated, Alex decided to follow the compass's direction, which led him through hidden alleys and forgotten streets of the city. His journey brought him to an abandoned warehouse, where he found a cryptic message left behind by a secret society. This message hinted at a hidden world within the city, waiting to be uncovered by someone brave enough.

5.6) What does the mysterious compass most likely symbolize in the story?

☐ A regular city tour

☐ Alex's homework challenges

☐ Alex's love for sports

☐ The adventure and mysteries of the city

5.7) How does the setting of Newhaven contribute to the story?

☐ It emphasizes the importance of family

☐ It provides a backdrop for nature exploration

☐ It highlights technological advancements

☐ It adds a sense of urban adventure and discovery

5.8) The author's use of 'hidden alleys' and 'forgotten streets' serves to:

☐ Add historical context

☐ Create a sense of familiarity

☐ Focus on urban development

☐ Build suspense and mystery

5.9) What narrative technique is used when describing Alex's journey through the city?

☐ First-person perspective

☐ Omniscient narration

☐ Detailed geographical explanation

☐ Objective reporting

5.10) The discovery of the cryptic message in the warehouse primarily adds which element to the story?

☐ Historical accuracy

☐ Everyday realism

☐ Comic relief

☐ An element of intrigue and potential danger

Sarah, a young aspiring artist, lived in a vibrant coastal town. One day, while walking along the beach, she discovered a colorful, ornate bottle half-buried in the sand. Inside, she found a series of paintings, each depicting different parts of her town in a unique, whimsical style. As Sarah examined these paintings, she began to notice subtle clues hinting at a hidden treasure. Intrigued, she decided to follow these clues, leading her on an artistic journey through her town's history and culture.

5.11) The ornate bottle and paintings most likely symbolize:

☐ A typical day at the beach

☐ Sarah's daily routine

☐ Sarah's love for the ocean

☐ A mystery waiting to be unraveled

5.12) How does the author use the paintings to enhance the story?

☐ By creating a historical context

☐ Through the clues in the paintings leading to a treasure

☐ By depicting different weather conditions

☐ By focusing on artistic techniques

5.13) Sarah's journey through the town's history adds what element to the narrative?

☐ A focus on modern life

☐ An emphasis on outdoor activities

☐ Technological advancement

☐ Cultural and historical depth

5.14) The setting of the vibrant coastal town contributes to the story by:

☐ Providing a backdrop for Sarah's art lessons

☐ Focusing on urban development

☐ Creating a colorful and lively atmosphere

☐ Teaching about marine life

5.15) The author's style in describing Sarah's adventure can best be described as:

☐ Formal and instructive

☐ Dry and factual

☐ Humorous and lighthearted

☐ Imaginative and engaging

In the enchanting forest of Greenwood, there lived a wise old owl named Oliver. Oliver was not just any owl; he had the ability to speak with humans. One evening, a young boy named Lucas, lost in the forest, stumbled upon Oliver. Oliver decided to guide Lucas, sharing tales of the forest's mysteries and magic. As they journeyed, Lucas discovered hidden paths and ancient ruins, learning about the forest's secrets and the importance of preserving nature.

5.16) What does Oliver the owl symbolize in the story?

☐ A common forest animal

☐ A guide and a source of wisdom

☐ The dangers of the forest

☐ Lucas's fear of being lost

5.17) How does the author use Oliver's tales to enhance the narrative?

☐ By teaching about different bird species

☐ By focusing on Lucas's home life

☐ Through the mysteries and magic of the forest

☐ By describing the forest's flora and fauna

5.18) Lucas's discovery of ancient ruins adds what element to the story?

☐ A focus on urban exploration

☐ Historical and mystical elements

☐ An insight into modern architecture

☐ An emphasis on sports and physical activity

5.19) The setting in the enchanting Greenwood forest contributes how to the story?

☐ Focusing on agricultural practices

☐ Providing a backdrop for technological advancements

☐ Teaching about city life

☐ Creating a magical and adventurous atmosphere

5.20) The author's style in depicting Lucas's adventure can best be described as:

□ Comical and entertaining

□ Straightforward and realistic

□ Captivating and imaginative

□ Technical and precise

In the bustling city of Harmony, a young musician named Ava discovered a mysterious, old piano in her attic. This piano had a unique design and seemed to play melodies on its own. Intrigued, Ava started playing it and found that the piano had magical powers – it could transport her to the world of the compositions she played. Each piece took her on a different journey, from the baroque era to futuristic soundscapes, teaching her not just about music, but about history, cultures, and emotions.

5.21) What does the magical piano symbolize in the story?

□ A regular instrument

□ Ava's love for modern technology

□ A gateway to musical and historical adventures

□ A family heirloom

5.22) How does the author use the piano's power to enhance the narrative?

□ By focusing on Ava's piano lessons

□ By describing the attic's appearance

□ Through the journeys to different musical eras

□ By highlighting Ava's school life

5.23) Ava's travels to different eras add what element to the story?

☐ A focus on contemporary music

☐ An emphasis on technology

☐ Historical and cultural depth

☐ A look at daily routines

5.24) The setting in the city of Harmony contributes how to the story?

☐ Providing a backdrop for urban adventures

☐ Creating a contrast to the magical experiences

☐ Teaching about city planning

☐ Focusing on outdoor activities

5.25) The author's style in depicting Ava's musical journeys can best be described as:

☐ Simple and straightforward

☐ Educational and factual

☐ Enchanting and imaginative

☐ Humorous and playful

In the mystical land of Eldoria, a young explorer named Leo found a crystal orb in an ancient temple. The orb, shimmering with multicolored lights, was said to hold the power to reveal hidden truths of the world. As Leo held the orb, visions of forgotten civilizations and untold stories filled his mind. He realized that the orb was a key to understanding the mysteries of Eldoria, leading him on a quest to uncover the secrets of the past and learn about the legends that shaped his world.

5.26) What does the crystal orb most likely symbolize in the story?

☐ A common toy

☐ A simple decoration

☐ A source of light

☐ A key to historical and mystical knowledge

5.27) How does the author use the visions to enhance the story?

☐ By focusing on Leo's daily routine

☐ By introducing a talking animal

☐ By describing the temple's architecture

☐ Through the revelations of forgotten civilizations

5.28) Leo's quest to uncover past secrets adds what element to the story?

☐ An emphasis on outdoor sports

☐ A look at urban life

☐ Historical and fantastical elements

☐ A focus on modern technology

5.29) The setting in the mystical land of Eldoria contributes how to the story?

☐ Focusing on agricultural practices

☐ Creating a magical and adventurous atmosphere

☐ Teaching about city life

☐ Providing a backdrop for technological advancements

5.30) The author's style in depicting Leo's journey can best be described as:

☐ Technical and precise

☐ Enchanting and imaginative

☐ Straightforward and realistic

☐ Humorous and entertaining

In a peaceful village surrounded by mountains, a girl named Zoe discovered a hidden garden behind her house. This garden was unlike any other, filled with exotic flowers and plants that glowed in the moonlight. Among the plants, Zoe found a rare flower that whispered secrets of the natural world. As she cared for the garden, she learned about the delicate balance of nature and the importance of preserving it, gaining a deeper connection with the environment around her.

5.31) What does the hidden garden symbolize in the story?

☐ A source of beauty and mystery

☐ A typical gardening area

☐ A regular backyard space

☐ A place for Zoe's outdoor games

5.32) How does the author use the rare flower to enhance the narrative?

☐ Through the secrets it whispers about nature

☐ By describing the other flowers

☐ By introducing a talking animal

☐ By focusing on gardening techniques

5.33) Zoe's connection with the environment adds what element to the story?

☐ Insight into environmental awareness and preservation

☐ An emphasis on technological advancements

☐ A focus on urban life

☐ A look at daily routines in the village

5.34) The setting in the village surrounded by mountains contributes how to the story?

☐ Focusing on industrial development

☐ Teaching about mountain climbing

☐ Creating a serene and natural atmosphere

☐ Providing a backdrop for urban adventures

5.35) The author's style in depicting Zoe's discovery can best be described as:

☐ Technical and factual

☐ Formal and instructive

☐ Humorous and light-hearted

☐ Whimsical and insightful

In a future world where people lived in floating cities above the clouds, a young inventor named Kai created a pair of extraordinary glasses that could see into the past. Wearing them, Kai could witness historical events and learn from the experiences of past generations. His first journey with the glasses took him back to the founding of the floating cities, revealing the challenges and triumphs of the people who built them. Kai's adventures gave him insights into the importance of learning from history to shape a better future.

5.36) What do Kai's extraordinary glasses most likely symbolize in the story?

□ A common toy

□ A tool for historical exploration and learning

□ A fashion accessory

□ An everyday object

5.37) How does the author use the time-travel aspect to enhance the narrative?

□ By introducing a talking animal

□ By describing the technology of the glasses

□ By focusing on Kai's daily life

□ Through Kai's experiences of historical events

5.38) Kai's journey to the founding of the floating cities adds what element to the story?

□ A look at daily routines in the cities

□ A focus on modern technology

□ Historical depth and perspective

□ An emphasis on sports and physical activity

5.39) The setting in the floating cities above the clouds contributes how to the story?

☐ Creating a futuristic and imaginative atmosphere

☐ Providing a backdrop for ground-level adventures

☐ Focusing on agricultural practices

☐ Teaching about traditional city planning

5.40) The author's style in depicting Kai's adventures can best be described as:

☐ Technical and detailed

☐ Humorous and lighthearted

☐ Innovative and thought-provoking

☐ Plain and straightforward

Topic 5 - Answers

Question Number	Answer	Explanation
5.1	An upcoming adventure of family discovery	Finding the well foreshadows Emily's adventure into her great-grandmother's past and the magical world.
5.2	Through the sudden discovery of the well and the diary	The unexpected discovery creates mystery and intrigue, drawing readers into the story.
5.3	Historical depth and magical allure	The diary introduces elements of history and magic, adding depth to the narrative.
5.4	It provides a mystical and adventurous atmosphere	Maplewood's description as a place of forests and streams sets a mystical and adventurous tone.
5.5	Mysterious and engaging	The author's tone is engaging and filled with mystery, captivating the reader.
5.6	The adventure and mysteries of the city	The compass symbolizes the hidden adventures and mysteries in the city.
5.7	It adds a sense of urban adventure and discovery	Newhaven's urban setting provides a backdrop for Alex's adventure and discovery.
5.8	Build suspense and mystery	The use of 'hidden alleys' and 'forgotten streets' adds a mysterious and suspenseful tone.
5.9	Omniscient narration	The story is told in a way that reveals the thoughts and experiences of the character, suggesting this style.
5.10	An element of intrigue and potential danger	The cryptic message adds a layer of mystery and hints at potential danger.
5.11	A mystery waiting to be unraveled	The bottle and paintings symbolize a hidden mystery and adventure in the story.
5.12	Through the clues in the paintings leading to a treasure	The paintings add to the narrative by providing clues that lead to a treasure.
5.13	Cultural and historical depth	Sarah's journey adds a cultural and historical perspective to the story.
5.14	Creating a colorful and lively atmosphere	The vibrant coastal town setting adds a lively and colorful backdrop to the story.
5.15	Imaginative and engaging	The author's style is imaginative, drawing readers into Sarah's artistic journey.
5.16	A guide and a source of wisdom	Oliver symbolizes guidance and wisdom in the forest's mysteries.
5.17	Through the mysteries and magic of the forest	Oliver's tales enhance the narrative by revealing the magic and mysteries of the forest.
5.18	Historical and mystical elements	The discovery of ancient ruins adds a historical and mystical aspect to the story.

5.19	Creating a magical and adventurous atmosphere	The enchanting forest setting provides a magical and adventurous backdrop.
5.20	Captivating and imaginative	The author's style is imaginative, capturing the magical journey of Lucas.
5.21	A gateway to musical and historical adventures	The magical piano symbolizes a portal to various historical and musical experiences.
5.22	Through the journeys to different musical eras	The piano's power enhances the narrative by taking Ava on journeys through different musical eras.
5.23	Historical and cultural depth	Ava's travels add a historical and cultural dimension to the story.
5.24	Creating a contrast to the magical experiences	The city setting contrasts with the magical experiences provided by the piano.
5.25	Enchanting and imaginative	The author's style is enchanting, drawing readers into the magical musical journeys.
5.26	A key to historical and mystical knowledge	The orb symbolizes a key to unlocking knowledge of the world's history and mysteries.
5.27	Through the revelations of forgotten civilizations	The visions enhance the narrative by revealing forgotten civilizations and stories.
5.28	Historical and fantastical elements	Leo's quest adds elements of history and fantasy to the story.
5.29	Creating a magical and adventurous atmosphere	Eldoria's setting provides a magical and adventurous backdrop for the story.
5.30	Enchanting and imaginative	The author's style is imaginative, drawing readers into Leo's mystical journey.
5.31	A source of beauty and mystery	The hidden garden symbolizes a mystical and beautiful world within the story.
5.32	Through the secrets it whispers about nature	The rare flower enhances the narrative by revealing secrets about nature.
5.33	Insight into environmental awareness and preservation	Zoe's connection with the environment adds an element of environmental awareness and preservation.
5.34	Creating a serene and natural atmosphere	The mountainous village setting creates a serene and natural atmosphere.
5.35	Whimsical and insightful	The author's style is whimsical, providing insight into Zoe's discovery and connection with nature.
5.36	A tool for historical exploration and learning	The glasses symbolize a means for Kai to explore and learn from history.
5.37	Through Kai's experiences of historical events	The time-travel aspect is used to enhance the narrative through Kai's historical experiences.
5.38	Historical depth and perspective	Kai's journey to the past adds historical depth and perspective to the story.
5.39	Creating a futuristic and imaginative atmosphere	The setting of floating cities adds a futuristic and imaginative element to the story.
5.40	Innovative and thought-provoking	The author's style is innovative, provoking thought about history and its impact on the future.

ALEXANDER-GRACE EDUCATION

Topic 6 – Dialogue and Conversation

In the small town of Pineville, two friends, Emma and Alex, stumbled upon an old, abandoned theater. Intrigued, they explored its dusty corridors and found a script of a play from long ago. As they read the script aloud, characters from the play magically appeared, conversing with Emma and Alex. Through these interactions, they learned about the theater's history and the importance of keeping arts alive in their community.

6.1) How does the dialogue with the play's characters help Emma and Alex understand the theater's history?

☐ It gives them a history lesson

☐ By talking about their hobbies

☐ By discussing modern technology

☐ Through stories from the past

6.2) What does the interaction between Emma and Alex reveal about their friendship?

☐ They don't like old theaters

☐ They prefer to stay at home

☐ They enjoy exploring

☐ They are afraid of plays

6.3) How do the characters from the play contribute to the story's theme of arts preservation?

☐ By discussing sports

☐ Through their tales and experiences

☐ By teaching them to paint

☐ By performing a dance

6.4) What role does the dialogue play in the children's adventure in the theater?

☐ It talks about their school

☐ It describes the theater's architecture

☐ It leads to a treasure hunt

☐ It focuses on cleaning the theater

6.5) Why is the conversation with the play's characters crucial for the story's magical element?

☐ It brings the past to life

☐ It describes the costumes

☐ It discusses stage lighting

☐ It focuses on ticket sales

On the outskirts of Greenwood, siblings Sara and Ryan discovered a talking tree named Willow in a hidden grove. Willow, wise and ancient, told them tales of the forest's past and secrets of the natural world. Through their dialogues, Sara and Ryan learned about environmental conservation and the interconnectedness of all living things, gaining a newfound respect for nature and its stories.

6.6) How does the conversation with Willow the tree enlighten Sara and Ryan about the forest?

☐ Through tales of the grove's history

☐ It gives a geography lesson

☐ By talking about gardening

☐ By discussing tree types

6.7) What does the dialogue between Sara and Ryan show about their interest in nature?

☐ They are nature experts

☐ They prefer city life

☐ They want to know more about it

☐ They like indoor activities

6.8) How does Willow's storytelling add to the environmental theme of the story?

☐ By offering gardening tips

☐ By discussing weather patterns

☐ By focusing on urban development

☐ Through insights on nature's balance

6.9) What role does the dialogue play in the siblings' discovery in the grove?

☐ It leads to a picnic

☐ It describes different birds

☐ It talks about sports

☐ It unveils the forest's secrets

6.10) Why is the conversation with Willow important for understanding the story's conservation message?

☐ It talks about hiking trails

☐ It discusses tree age

☐ It focuses on logging practices

☐ It emphasizes interconnectedness

In the bustling city of Starpoint, two classmates, Lily and Ethan, joined a school play. During rehearsals, they found an old diary in the theater's attic, which belonged to a famous actress from decades ago. As they read the diary, they began to understand the actress's journey, her challenges, and her passion for theater. This discovery inspired them to put extra effort into their roles, learning not just their lines, but also the emotions and motivations behind them, leading to a deeper appreciation of theatrical arts.

6.11) What does the old diary reveal about the famous actress?

☐ Her vacation destinations

☐ Her favorite color

☐ Her journey and passion for theater

☐ Her favorite foods

6.12) How does the dialogue in the play help Lily and Ethan in their roles?

☐ By understanding emotions and motivations

☐ By focusing on their hobbies

☐ It teaches them about fashion

☐ By discussing modern technology

6.13) What does the interaction between Lily and Ethan show about their approach to acting?

☐ They are dedicated and thoughtful

☐ They are not interested in acting

☐ They like to skip rehearsals

☐ They prefer to improvise

6.14) How does the diary's content enhance the theme of the story?

☐ By offering acting tips

☐ Through insights into the actress's life

☐ By discussing different theater styles

☐ By focusing on set design

6.15) Why is the discovery of the diary crucial for Lily and Ethan's growth in the play?

☐ It focuses on audience management

☐ It inspires and guides their performance

☐ It describes the theater's architecture

☐ It talks about lighting techniques

In the village of Greenfield, during a summer camp, two friends, Noah and Sophie, decided to write a play about their adventures. They created characters based on their fellow campers and included events from their camp experiences. As they wrote dialogues, they explored different perspectives, learning more about their friends' thoughts and feelings. This process not only brought them closer to their peers but also taught them the value of empathy and understanding.

6.16) How do the dialogues in Noah and Sophie's play reflect their camp experiences?

☐ Through events and characters based on real experiences

☐ By talking about video games

☐ By discussing camp food

☐ By focusing on the weather

6.17) What does the writing process reveal about Noah and Sophie's friendship?

☐ They don't work well together

☐ They are not interested in writing

☐ They prefer to work alone

☐ They collaborate and value each other's ideas

6.18) How do the play's characters contribute to understanding different perspectives?

☐ By performing dance routines

☐ By focusing on sports activities

☐ Through dialogues reflecting diverse thoughts and feelings

☐ By discussing fashion trends

6.19) What role does the dialogue play in the campers' connection in the story?

☐ It describes the camping gear

☐ It leads to a cooking competition

☐ It talks about their favorite TV shows

☐ It fosters empathy and bonding

6.20) Why is the process of writing the play important for Noah and Sophie's personal growth?

☐ It focuses on lighting techniques

☐ It discusses audience management

☐ It enhances their empathy and understanding of others

☐ It teaches them about stage design

In the bustling city of Metroville, a group of students in Ms. Parker's class decided to create a podcast. They planned to interview people from their neighborhood, sharing stories and experiences. As they conversed with a variety of individuals, from the local baker to the librarian, they uncovered the rich tapestry of their community's history and diversity. This project not only taught them about effective communication but also the power of listening to others' stories.

6.21) What do the interviews in the podcast reveal about the neighborhood?

☐ The latest fashion trends

☐ Its preference for certain sports

☐ The students' favorite video games

☐ The diversity and history of the community

6.22) How does the dialogue during the interviews show the students' learning process?

☐ They develop communication and listening skills

☐ They focus on technology

☐ They learn about baking and librarianship

☐ They discuss their homework

6.23) What role do the varied perspectives in the podcast play in the narrative?

☐ They offer cooking tips

☐ They focus on shopping experiences

☐ They enrich the understanding of community life

☐ They discuss TV shows

6.24) How does the podcast project enhance the students' connection with their community?

☐ It fosters appreciation and engagement

☐ It leads to a sports competition

☐ It describes the city's architecture

☐ It talks about public transport

6.25) Why is the process of creating the podcast important for the students' development?

□ It focuses on technical aspects of podcasting

□ It cultivates empathy and broadens their worldview

□ It discusses audience demographics

□ It teaches them about sound editing

In the historical town of Rivertown, a group of children decided to create a time capsule. To decide what to include, they interviewed older residents to learn about the town's past. Each interview brought fascinating stories of different eras, highlighting changes and constants in the community's life. This journey through time, facilitated by conversations with the elders, allowed the children to appreciate their heritage and understand the importance of preserving memories for future generations.

6.26) What do the interviews with older residents reveal about Rivertown?

□ The rich history and transformations of the town

□ Current fashion trends

□ Its sports teams

□ The latest technology gadgets

6.27) How does the dialogue in the interviews show the children's curiosity?

□ They are eager to learn about the town's past

□ They discuss their school subjects

□ They ask about video games

□ They talk about their favorite TV shows

ALEXANDER-GRACE EDUCATION

6.28) What role do the elders' stories play in the narrative?

☐ They offer cooking recipes

☐ They discuss modern architecture

☐ They provide a connection to the town's history

☐ They focus on gardening tips

6.29) How does creating the time capsule enhance the children's sense of community?

☐ It talks about local shops

☐ It describes the town's buildings

☐ It leads to a neighborhood party

☐ It fosters a sense of belonging and continuity

6.30) Why is the project of making a time capsule important for the children's growth?

☐ It helps them understand the value of history and memory

☐ It teaches them about container design

☐ It focuses on excavation techniques

☐ It discusses environmental conservation

In the small town of Maplewood, a group of friends started a community newspaper. To gather stories, they interviewed various townspeople, from the local baker to the mayor. Each interviewee shared unique insights about life in Maplewood, from historical events to everyday joys and challenges. The friends' conversations with these individuals not only filled the pages of their newspaper but also deepened their understanding of the community's spirit.

6.31) What do the interviews for the newspaper reveal about Maplewood?

☐ Popular video games in town

☐ Diverse perspectives and experiences of the townspeople

☐ The latest fashion trends

☐ Details about sports activities

6.32) How does the dialogue in the interviews show the friends' engagement with the community?

☐ They talk about technology gadgets

☐ They focus on their hobbies

☐ They actively listen and learn about the townspeople's lives

☐ They discuss their favorite TV shows

6.33) What role do the townspeople's stories play in the narrative of the newspaper?

☐ They provide cooking recipes

☐ They discuss modern architecture

☐ They focus on home decoration tips

☐ They add depth and richness to the community's portrayal

6.34) How does creating the community newspaper enhance the friends' connection to Maplewood?

☐ It describes the town's landscape

☐ It talks about local entertainment options

☐ It leads to a sports event

☐ It fosters a sense of belonging and involvement

6.35) Why is the project of the community newspaper important for the friends' development?

☐ It helps them appreciate the value of community narratives

☐ It focuses on journalistic ethics

☐ It discusses advertising strategies

☐ It teaches them about printing techniques

In the vibrant neighborhood of Lakeside, a group of young students formed a drama club. Their first project was to create an original play based on the stories of their families. Each member interviewed their family members, gathering tales of their heritage, traditions, and personal journeys. These narratives were woven into the play, showcasing the rich tapestry of cultures and experiences that made up their community, and teaching the students the importance of storytelling.

6.36) What do the family stories gathered for the play reveal about the students' community?

☐ The local fashion trends

☐ The popular restaurants

☐ The diversity and richness of cultural backgrounds

☐ The favorite sports teams

6.37) How does the dialogue in the play show the family histories?

☐ Through authentic representations of heritage and traditions

☐ It focuses on modern lifestyles

☐ It talks about holiday destinations

☐ It discusses technological advancements

6.38) What role do the various narratives play in the drama club's play?

☐ They focus on fitness routines

☐ They provide cooking recipes

☐ They bring depth and connectivity to the community portrayal

☐ They discuss academic achievements

6.39) How does creating the play enhance the students' sense of identity and community?

☐ It talks about recreational facilities

☐ It fosters appreciation of their diverse backgrounds

☐ It leads to a sports event

☐ It describes the town's infrastructure

6.40) Why is the project of writing and performing the play important for the students' personal growth?

☐ It helps them value storytelling and understand diverse perspectives

☐ It discusses audience management

☐ It focuses on acting techniques

☐ It teaches them about stage lighting

Topic 6 - Answers

Question Number	Answer	Explanation
6.1	Through stories from the past	The characters from the play provide historical insights through their stories.
6.2	They enjoy exploring	Their exploration of the theater shows their shared interest and adventurous spirit.
6.3	Through their tales and experiences	The characters from the play highlight the importance of arts through their personal stories.
6.4	It leads to a treasure hunt	The dialogue guides them on an adventure, akin to a treasure hunt, within the theater.
6.5	It brings the past to life	The conversation with the characters magically animates the past, adding a magical element.
6.6	Through tales of the grove's history	Willow's stories educate the siblings about the forest's history and secrets.
6.7	They want to know more about it	Their conversations with Willow show their curiosity and eagerness to learn about nature.
6.8	Through insights on nature's balance	Willow's stories add to the environmental theme by teaching about nature's balance.
6.9	It unveils the forest's secrets	The dialogue with Willow reveals secrets and knowledge about the forest.
6.10	It emphasizes interconnectedness	Willow's conversation underscores the interconnectedness of nature, reinforcing the conservation message.
6.11	Her journey and passion for theater	The diary provides insight into the actress's journey and her passion for theater.
6.12	By understanding emotions and motivations	The dialogue helps Lily and Ethan understand the underlying emotions and motivations in acting.
6.13	They are dedicated and thoughtful	Their interaction during rehearsals shows their dedication and thoughtfulness towards acting.
6.14	Through insights into the actress's life	The diary's content adds depth to the theme by providing a glimpse into the actress's life.
6.15	It inspires and guides their performance	The discovery of the diary inspires Lily and Ethan and guides their performance in the play.
6.16	Through events and characters based on real experiences	The play reflects their real camp experiences through its characters and events.
6.17	They collaborate and value each other's ideas	Their writing process shows they work well together and value each other's contributions.
6.18	Through dialogues reflecting diverse thoughts and feelings	The characters in their play help in understanding different perspectives through dialogues.

6.19	It fosters empathy and bonding	The dialogue in their play helps in building empathy and stronger bonds among the campers.
6.20	It enhances their empathy and understanding of others	Writing the play helps Noah and Sophie grow personally by enhancing their empathy and understanding.
6.21	The diversity and history of the community	The interviews in the podcast reveal the rich diversity and history of the community.
6.22	They develop communication and listening skills	The dialogue during interviews shows the students' growth in communication and listening skills.
6.23	They enrich the understanding of community life	The varied perspectives in the podcast enrich the narrative and understanding of community life.
6.24	It fosters appreciation and engagement	Creating the podcast enhances the students' connection and engagement with their community.
6.25	It cultivates empathy and broadens their worldview	The podcast creation process is important for developing empathy and a broadened worldview.
6.26	The rich history and transformations of the town	The interviews with older residents reveal the town's rich history and transformations.
6.27	They are eager to learn about the town's past	The dialogue shows the children's curiosity and eagerness to learn about the town's past.
6.28	They provide a connection to the town's history	The elders' stories play a crucial role in connecting the narrative to the town's history.
6.29	It fosters a sense of belonging and continuity	Creating the time capsule enhances the children's sense of community belonging and historical continuity.
6.30	It helps them understand the value of history and memory	The time capsule project is important for the children's understanding of history and memory.
6.31	Diverse perspectives and experiences of the townspeople	The interviews for the newspaper reveal diverse perspectives and experiences in Maplewood.
6.32	They actively listen and learn about the townspeople's lives	The dialogue shows the friends' active engagement and learning about the lives of townspeople.
6.33	They add depth and richness to the community's portrayal	The townspeople's stories add depth and richness to the newspaper's portrayal of the community.
6.34	It fosters a sense of belonging and involvement	Creating the newspaper enhances the friends' connection and involvement in Maplewood.
6.35	It helps them appreciate the value of community narratives	The newspaper project is important for appreciating community narratives and their own development.
6.36	The diversity and richness of cultural backgrounds	The family stories reveal the diversity and richness of the students' community's cultural backgrounds.
6.37	Through authentic representations of heritage and traditions	The dialogue in the play reflects the members' family histories through authentic representation.
6.38	They bring depth and connectivity to the community portrayal	The various narratives in the play bring depth and connectivity to the portrayal of the community.
6.39	It fosters appreciation of their diverse backgrounds	Creating the play enhances the students' appreciation for their diverse backgrounds and community.
6.40	It helps them value storytelling and understand diverse perspectives	Writing and performing the play is important for valuing storytelling and understanding diversity.

Topic 7 – Evaluating Conflict and Resolution

In the magical forest of Everwood, a young girl named Ellie discovered a lost kitten. The kitten, named Whiskers, belonged to the forest's guardian, a wise owl. As Ellie tried to return Whiskers, she faced various challenges, such as crossing a tricky river and finding the owl's hidden home. Along the way, Ellie learned about courage, friendship, and problem-solving. In the end, she successfully overcame these obstacles and reunited Whiskers with the guardian owl.

7.1) What is the main conflict Ellie faces in the story?

☐ Returning Whiskers to the guardian owl

☐ Choosing a new pet

☐ Finding a place to play

☐ Deciding what to wear

7.2) How does crossing the tricky river add to the story's climax?

☐ It is an unrelated event

☐ It is a time for a picnic

☐ It is a moment of relaxation

☐ It presents a significant challenge for Ellie

7.3) What does Ellie learn through resolving the conflict?

☐ Facts about owls

☐ Rules of a board game

☐ Courage and problem-solving

☐ How to cook

7.4) How is the conflict of finding the owl's home resolved?

☐ By going back home

☐ By asking a passing bird

☐ Through Ellie's determination and clever thinking

☐ It remains unsolved

7.5) What part of the story represents the resolution?

☐ The reunion of Whiskers with the guardian owl

☐ The beginning

☐ Crossing the river

☐ When Ellie first finds Whiskers

In the bustling city of Brightville, a boy named Leo found an ancient treasure map in his attic. The map led to a hidden gem in the city park. As Leo embarked on this adventure, he encountered various challenges, such as deciphering clues and avoiding mischievous rivals. Throughout his journey, Leo learned about perseverance, teamwork, and creative thinking. Eventually, Leo and his friends outwitted their rivals and discovered the hidden gem, learning valuable lessons about trust and friendship.

7.6) What is the main conflict in Leo's adventure?

☐ Learning a new sport

☐ Finding the hidden gem in the city park

☐ Choosing a game to play

☐ Deciding what to eat for lunch

7.7) How does avoiding the rivals add to the story's tension?

☐ It is a time for rest

☐ It introduces additional challenges for Leo

☐ It is a fun and relaxing moment

☐ It is an unrelated side story

7.8) What does Leo learn through overcoming the challenges?

☐ Perseverance and teamwork

☐ Rules of a computer game

☐ Tips for gardening

☐ How to play chess

7.9) How is the conflict of deciphering the clues resolved?

☐ Through Leo's creative thinking and collaboration

☐ The clues remain a mystery

☐ By asking a teacher for help

☐ By ignoring them

7.10) What part of the story represents the resolution?

☐ Reading the treasure map

☐ The finding of the hidden gem

☐ The start of the treasure hunt

☐ The discovery of the attic

In the quiet town of Meadowvale, a girl named Ava and her dog, Buster, found a mysterious key in their backyard. Curious about its origin, they embarked on a quest to find the lock it opened. Their adventure led them to various locations in town, facing obstacles like deciphering riddles and navigating unfamiliar paths. Through these challenges, Ava learned about resourcefulness, bravery, and the importance of curiosity. Eventually, Ava and Buster discovered an old chest in the local library, unlocking secrets from the town's history.

7.11) What is the main conflict in Ava's quest?

☐ Choosing a new pet

☐ Learning a musical instrument

☐ Finding the lock for the mysterious key

☐ Deciding on a birthday gift

7.12) How do the riddles add to the story's intrigue?

☐ They are simple and straightforward

☐ They provide challenging clues for Ava to solve

☐ They are unrelated to the key

☐ They offer a chance to rest

7.13) What does Ava learn by navigating the unfamiliar paths?

☐ Tips for baking cookies

☐ How to play soccer

☐ Resourcefulness and bravery

☐ Names of different plants

7.14) How is the conflict of finding the right lock resolved?

☐ Through determination and exploration

☐ By asking for help from a friend

☐ The lock remains undiscovered

☐ By giving up on the search

7.15) What part of the story represents the resolution?

☐ Reading books about keys

☐ The journey through the town

☐ Unlocking the old chest in the library

☐ When they first find the key

In the bustling suburb of Willow Creek, two siblings, Jake and Emma, discovered a mysterious puzzle box at a garage sale. Upon trying to solve it, they realized it was magically locked, and the key to open it was solving riddles hidden around their neighborhood. Their quest to solve the riddles led them to various local landmarks, where they faced challenges and met new friends. This adventure taught them about collaboration, ingenuity, and the history of their community. In the end, they solved the puzzle box, revealing a message about the importance of unity and community spirit.

7.16) What is the main conflict Jake and Emma face?

☐ Solving the puzzle box and its riddles

☐ Learning a new sport

☐ Choosing a game to play

☐ Deciding what to have for dinner

7.17) How do the hidden riddles add to the story's suspense?

☐ They are easy and quick to solve

☐ They are irrelevant to the puzzle

☐ They provide challenging and mysterious tasks

☐ They offer moments of relaxation

7.18) What do Jake and Emma learn by solving the riddles?

☐ Collaboration and ingenuity

☐ How to cook new recipes

☐ Tips for gardening

☐ Basics of computer programming

7.19) How is the conflict of the magically locked box resolved?

☐ Through teamwork and solving all the riddles

☐ By asking for help from a friend

☐ By breaking it open

☐ The box remains locked

7.20) What part of the story represents the resolution?

☐ The final opening of the puzzle box

☐ The visit to local landmarks

☐ The initial discovery of the box

☐ Reading books about puzzles

In the coastal town of Seaview, a group of children found a mysterious map leading to an abandoned lighthouse. The lighthouse was rumored to be haunted, and the map indicated a hidden treasure inside. Overcoming their fears, the children decided to explore the lighthouse. They encountered spooky sounds and illusions, but worked together to uncover the truth. Their journey taught them about courage, teamwork, and the value of curiosity. In the end, they discovered the 'treasure' was a time capsule left by the town's founders, filled with historical artifacts.

7.21) What is the main conflict the children face in the story?

☐ Deciding on a snack

☐ Choosing a team sport to play

☐ Finding a lost pet

☐ Exploring the haunted lighthouse for treasure

7.22) How do the spooky sounds in the lighthouse add to the story's tension?

☐ They offer comic relief

☐ They are unrelated to the adventure

☐ They create a spooky and mysterious atmosphere

☐ They are calming and pleasant

7.23) What do the children learn from their adventure in the lighthouse?

☐ Basics of sailing

☐ Tips for baking

☐ How to swim

☐ Courage, teamwork, and curiosity

7.24) How is the conflict of the haunted lighthouse resolved?

☐ By calling the police

☐ Through bravery and uncovering the time capsule

☐ The lighthouse remains a mystery

☐ By asking for help from adults

7.25) What part of the story represents the resolution?

☐ The initial discovery of the map

☐ The approach to the lighthouse

☐ Finding the time capsule with historical artifacts

☐ Hearing the spooky sounds

In the mystical forest of Eldergrove, a young boy named Max discovered a talking tree named Eldrin. Eldrin told Max about a looming threat to the forest due to a magical disturbance. Determined to save Eldergrove, Max embarked on a quest to restore balance. He faced challenges like navigating enchanted mazes and solving ancient puzzles. Through his journey, Max learned about bravery, wisdom, and the importance of nature's harmony. Eventually, Max resolved the disturbance, restoring peace and vitality to Eldergrove.

7.26) What is the main conflict in Max's adventure?

☐ Learning to ride a bike

☐ Restoring balance to the mystical forest

☐ Finding a lost toy

☐ Choosing a new game to play

7.27) How do the enchanted mazes add to the story's climax?

☐ They are easy and straightforward

☐ They provide a relaxing break

☐ They present significant obstacles for Max

☐ They offer moments of comedy

7.28) What does Max learn from solving the ancient puzzles?

☐ How to solve math problems

☐ Basics of drawing

☐ Wisdom and the value of perseverance

☐ Tips for gardening

7.29) How is the magical disturbance in the forest resolved?

☐ The disturbance continues

☐ Through Max's bravery and wisdom

☐ By asking for help from a wizard

☐ By ignoring it

7.30) What part of the story represents the resolution?

☐ When Max first meets Eldrin

☐ Solving the first puzzle

☐ Navigating the mazes

☐ Restoring peace and vitality to the forest

In the bustling city of Sunridge, two friends, Hannah and Zoe, decided to build a community garden. However, they faced opposition from a local developer who wanted to build a shopping center on the same land. Determined to protect the green space, Hannah and Zoe organized community meetings, created petitions, and spoke at city council gatherings. Through their efforts, they learned about activism, community engagement, and environmental preservation. Ultimately, they managed to convince the council to preserve the land for the garden.

7.31) What is the main conflict in Hannah and Zoe's story?

☐ Protecting the land for a community garden

☐ Finding a lost pet

☐ Deciding on a weekend activity

☐ Choosing a new school

7.32) How do the community meetings add to the story's development?

☐ They offer moments of comedy

☐ They focus on leisure activities

☐ They are casual and unrelated

☐ They provide a platform for activism and engagement

7.33) What do Hannah and Zoe learn from their experience?

☐ How to bake cookies

☐ Activism, community engagement, and environmental preservation

☐ Basics of painting

☐ Tips for online gaming

7.34) How is the conflict with the developer resolved?

☐ The land is developed into a shopping center

☐ Through persuasive efforts and community support

☐ By asking for help from a celebrity

☐ By giving up the garden idea

7.35) What part of the story represents the resolution?

☐ Speaking at city council meetings

☐ Convincing the council to preserve the land

☐ The initial idea of the garden

☐ Organizing the petitions

In the adventurous town of Pine Peaks, a group of children discovered an old, abandoned mansion on the edge of town. Rumors said it was haunted, and the kids decided to explore it to uncover the truth. Inside, they encountered mysterious clues and eerie occurrences that tested their bravery. Working together, they solved puzzles and unveiled the mansion's history, learning about the power of teamwork and facing fears. Ultimately, they discovered the 'hauntings' were just tricks set up by a local inventor, and the mansion was actually a historical treasure.

7.36) What is the main conflict in the children's adventure?

☐ Finding the way to school

☐ Uncovering the truth about the haunted mansion

☐ Picking a movie to watch

☐ Choosing a game to play

7.37) How do the eerie occurrences add to the story's suspense?

☐ They are irrelevant to the mansion

☐ They create a spooky and thrilling atmosphere

☐ They offer moments of relaxation

☐ They are funny and entertaining

7.38) What do the children learn by exploring the mansion?

☐ How to cook

☐ Tips for gardening

☐ Teamwork and facing fears

☐ Basics of programming

7.39) How is the mystery of the haunted mansion resolved?

☐ Through solving puzzles and revealing it's not haunted

☐ The mansion remains a mystery

☐ By calling the police

☐ By avoiding the mansion

7.40) What part of the story represents the resolution?

☐ Finding the mansion

☐ Solving the first puzzle

☐ Revealing the inventor's tricks

☐ Entering the mansion

Topic 7 – Answers

Question Number	Answer	Explanation
7.1	Returning Whiskers to the guardian owl	The main conflict Ellie faces is the challenge of returning Whiskers to the owl.
7.2	It presents a significant challenge for Ellie	Crossing the river adds a climactic challenge for Ellie, heightening the story's tension.
7.3	Courage and problem-solving	Ellie learns about courage and problem-solving while resolving the conflicts she encounters.
7.4	Through Ellie's determination and clever thinking	The conflict of finding the owl's home is resolved through Ellie's determination and intelligence.
7.5	The reunion of Whiskers with the guardian owl	The story resolves with the successful reunion of Whiskers and the guardian owl.
7.6	Finding the hidden gem in the city park	Leo's main conflict is the quest to find the hidden gem in the city park.
7.7	It introduces additional challenges for Leo	Avoiding rivals adds tension and challenges to Leo's adventure.
7.8	Perseverance and teamwork	Leo learns about perseverance and teamwork through overcoming the challenges.
7.9	Through Leo's creative thinking and collaboration	Leo and his friends decipher the clues through creative thinking and teamwork.
7.10	The finding of the hidden gem	The resolution is marked by finding the hidden gem in the park.
7.11	Finding the lock for the mysterious key	Ava's main conflict is to find the lock that fits the mysterious key she found.
7.12	They provide challenging clues for Ava to solve	The riddles add intrigue by providing Ava with challenging clues to solve.
7.13	Resourcefulness and bravery	Ava learns resourcefulness and bravery as she navigates through unfamiliar paths.
7.14	Through determination and exploration	The conflict is resolved as Ava finds the right lock through exploration and determination.
7.15	Unlocking the old chest in the library	The resolution occurs when Ava unlocks the chest in the library, revealing the town's secrets.
7.16	Solving the puzzle box and its riddles	Jake and Emma's main conflict is solving the mysteriously locked puzzle box.
7.17	They provide challenging and mysterious tasks	The hidden riddles add suspense by posing challenging and mysterious tasks to solve.
7.18	Collaboration and ingenuity	By solving the riddles, Jake and Emma learn about collaboration and ingenuity.

7.19	Through teamwork and solving all the riddles	The puzzle box is unlocked through teamwork and solving all the associated riddles.
7.20	The final opening of the puzzle box	The resolution is represented by the final opening of the puzzle box.
7.21	Exploring the haunted lighthouse for treasure	The children's main conflict is exploring the haunted lighthouse to find the hidden treasure.
7.22	They create a spooky and mysterious atmosphere	The spooky sounds in the lighthouse add tension by creating a mysterious atmosphere.
7.23	Courage, teamwork, and curiosity	From their adventure, the children learn about courage, teamwork, and the value of curiosity.
7.24	Through bravery and uncovering the time capsule	The conflict is resolved when the children bravely uncover the time capsule in the lighthouse.
7.25	Finding the time capsule with historical artifacts	The resolution is the discovery of the time capsule filled with historical artifacts.
7.26	Restoring balance to the mystical forest	Max's main conflict is to restore balance to the mystical forest of Eldergrove.
7.27	They present significant obstacles for Max	The enchanted mazes add to the climax by presenting significant challenges for Max to overcome.
7.28	Wisdom and the value of perseverance	Max learns about wisdom and the importance of perseverance while solving ancient puzzles.
7.29	Through Max's bravery and wisdom	The magical disturbance is resolved through Max's bravery and wisdom.
7.30	Restoring peace and vitality to the forest	The resolution is represented by Max restoring peace and vitality to Eldergrove.
7.31	Protecting the land for a community garden	The main conflict is the struggle to protect land for a community garden against a developer.
7.32	They provide a platform for activism and engagement	The community meetings contribute to the story by enabling activism and community engagement.
7.33	Activism, community engagement, and environmental preservation	Hannah and Zoe learn about activism, community engagement, and environmental preservation.
7.34	Through persuasive efforts and community support	The conflict with the developer is resolved through community support and persuasive efforts.
7.35	Convincing the council to preserve the land	The resolution is achieved when the council is convinced to preserve the land for the garden.
7.36	Uncovering the truth about the haunted mansion	The children's main conflict is to discover the truth behind the rumored haunted mansion.
7.37	They create a spooky and thrilling atmosphere	The eerie occurrences add suspense by creating a spooky and thrilling atmosphere in the mansion.
7.38	Teamwork and facing fears	The children learn about teamwork and how to face their fears while exploring the mansion.
7.39	Through solving puzzles and revealing it's not haunted	The mystery of the haunted mansion is solved by uncovering the truth behind the eerie occurrences.
7.40	Revealing the inventor's tricks	The resolution is marked by the revelation that the hauntings were tricks by a local inventor.

Topic 8 - Critical Reading and Inference Making

In a small village named Green Meadows, a group of children discovered an old map leading to a secret garden. Throughout their journey, they encountered various challenges and learned about friendship, courage, and the joy of discovery. Their adventure was filled with riddles and surprises, but together they found the garden and turned it into a beautiful place for everyone.

8.1) What is the main idea of the story?

☐ Building a treehouse

☐ A school competition

☐ A birthday party

☐ The discovery of a secret garden

8.2) How does the secret garden contribute to the story?

☐ As the main destination of the children's adventure

☐ As a place for a picnic

☐ As a background setting

☐ As a place to play sports

8.3) What theme is explored through the children's journey?

☐ Friendship and adventure

☐ The importance of technology

☐ Learning mathematics

☐ Cooking skills

8.4) What challenge do the children face in the story?

☐ Finding a lost pet

☐ Completing homework

☐ Winning a race

☐ Solving riddles

8.5) What is the outcome of the children's adventure?

☐ They transform the garden

☐ They find a treasure

☐ They win a prize

☐ They go back home

In the city of Starville, a young girl named Lily and her friends decided to organize a neighborhood cleanup. They noticed the local park was littered and needed care. Throughout their cleanup, they discovered the importance of environmental conservation and community involvement. They faced challenges like coordinating the event and motivating others, but their determination led to a successful cleanup. The experience taught them about leadership, teamwork, and the impact of community service.

8.6) What is the main focus of Lily's story?

☐ Planning a birthday party

☐ Studying for a test

☐ Winning a sports competition

☐ Organizing a neighborhood cleanup

8.7) How does the condition of the park contribute to the story?

☐ As a venue for a concert

☐ It motivates the cleanup effort

☐ As a place for relaxation

☐ As a background setting

8.8) What theme is explored through the cleanup activity?

☐ Learning a new language

☐ Cooking recipes

☐ The fun of playing games

☐ Environmental conservation and community

8.9) What challenge do Lily and her friends face?

☐ Coordinating the event

☐ Finding a lost pet

☐ Completing a school project

☐ Practicing for a dance recital

8.10) What is the outcome of their efforts?

☐ They open a small business

☐ They start a new sports team

☐ The park remains the same

☐ The successful cleanup of the park

In the mountain town of Alpine Ridge, a group of students embarked on a project to learn about local wildlife. They set out on nature hikes, observed animals in their habitats, and kept detailed journals of their findings. Their exploration revealed the diversity of wildlife and the importance of preserving their habitats. The students faced challenges such as identifying animal tracks and understanding animal behavior, but their perseverance led to a deeper appreciation for nature and environmental stewardship.

8.11) What is the main topic of the students' project?

☐ Planning a community festival

☐ Preparing for a sports event

☐ Practicing for a music concert

☐ Learning about local wildlife

8.12) How do the nature hikes contribute to the story?

☐ As leisure activities

☐ They provide opportunities for wildlife observation

☐ As settings for picnics

☐ As unrelated events

8.13) What theme is highlighted by their exploration?

☐ The excitement of outdoor sports

☐ The importance of physical exercise

☐ The fun of camping

☐ Wildlife diversity and habitat preservation

8.14) What challenges do the students encounter?

☐ Learning to cook outdoors

☐ Navigating the hiking trails

☐ Identifying animal tracks and behaviors

☐ Finding the right camping gear

8.15) What is the outcome of their project?

☐ A deeper appreciation for nature

☐ They start a hiking club

☐ The wildlife remains a mystery

☐ They build a new playground

In the coastal village of Sandy Shores, a group of children decided to learn about sea life by visiting the local aquarium. During their visit, they observed different marine creatures and learned about their habitats and behaviors. They faced challenges like understanding complex ecosystems and the impact of pollution on marine life. This visit sparked their interest in marine biology and the importance of protecting ocean life.

8.16) What is the primary focus of the children's visit to the aquarium?

☐ Finding a lost item

☐ Preparing for a swimming competition

☐ Playing games on the beach

☐ Exploring sea life and learning about marine creatures

8.17) How does observing marine creatures add to the story?

□ It serves as a fun activity

□ It is a backdrop for their playtime

□ It educates them about marine habitats and behaviors

□ It is unrelated to their project

8.18) What theme emerges from their exploration of the aquarium?

□ The fun of beach activities

□ The importance of vacationing

□ The excitement of water sports

□ The complexity of marine ecosystems and conservation

8.19) What challenges do the children face during their visit?

□ Learning to swim

□ Finding the right aquarium exhibits

□ Choosing snacks at the cafeteria

□ Understanding ecosystems and pollution's impact

8.20) What is the outcome of their aquarium visit?

□ They leave without learning anything

□ They organize a beach party

□ They start a beach cleaning project

□ Increased interest in marine biology and conservation

In the bustling city of Brightvale, a young boy named Tim discovered an old, forgotten library in his neighborhood. Curious, he ventured inside and found a world of books covering various subjects. Tim was fascinated by the stories and facts he uncovered, learning about history, science, and different cultures. His exploration of the library taught him about the power of knowledge and the joy of learning. He shared this discovery with his friends, and they began regular visits, turning the library into a hub of learning and adventure.

8.21) What is the central focus of Tim's story?

☐ Competing in a school contest

☐ Playing sports in the park

☐ Visiting a friend's house

☐ Exploring an old library and learning from books

8.22) How does the discovery of the library contribute to the story?

☐ It is a place for Tim to rest

☐ It is a setting for a party

☐ It serves as a background for a game

☐ It initiates Tim's journey of learning and discovery

8.23) What theme is evident from Tim's exploration?

☐ The fun of outdoor activities

☐ The importance of technology

☐ The excitement of traveling

☐ The value of knowledge and learning

8.24) What does Tim learn from his visits to the library?

☐ Basic computer skills

☐ Tips for gardening

☐ How to cook

☐ About history, science, and cultures

8.25) What is the outcome of Tim's discovery of the library?

☐ The library remains unused

☐ It is converted into a museum

☐ It is demolished for a new building

☐ It becomes a center for learning for Tim and his friends

In the small town of Riverview, a group of friends started a project to learn about local history. They visited historical landmarks, interviewed long-time residents, and explored the town museum. Through their journey, they uncovered stories of the town's founding, important events, and notable figures. This exploration deepened their understanding of their community's past and its influence on the present. The friends shared their findings in a school presentation, sparking interest in local history among their peers.

8.26) What is the main subject of the friends' project?

☐ Planning a community festival

☐ Organizing a sports event

☐ Preparing for a music concert

☐ Learning about local history

8.27) How do the visits to historical landmarks contribute to the story?

☐ They serve as places for picnics

☐ They are unrelated to the project

☐ As venues for entertainment

☐ They help uncover the town's past

8.28) What theme emerges from their historical exploration?

☐ The fun of camping

☐ The excitement of outdoor sports

☐ The richness of local history and its impact

☐ The importance of technology

8.29) What do the friends learn from their project?

☐ Tips for gardening

☐ How to cook

☐ Stories of the town's founding and notable figures

☐ Basics of computer programming

8.30) What is the outcome of their research on local history?

☐ They open a small cafe

☐ A school presentation inspiring interest in history

☐ They build a new playground

☐ They start a gardening club

In the vibrant neighborhood of Sunnyside, a group of children created an art exhibit showcasing their community's culture. They gathered artwork from local artists, including paintings, sculptures, and photographs. The exhibit displayed the diverse backgrounds, traditions, and stories of Sunnyside's residents. Through organizing the exhibit, the children learned about artistic expression, cultural diversity, and community pride. The event was a success, drawing attention from the wider community and fostering a sense of unity.

8.31) What is the central activity in the children's story?

☐ Setting up a science fair

☐ Creating an art exhibit

☐ Playing a basketball tournament

☐ Organizing a music festival

8.32) How does the artwork contribute to the story?

☐ It showcases the community's culture

☐ It serves as a backdrop for the story

☐ It is unrelated to the exhibit

☐ As decorative items

8.33) What theme is highlighted through the art exhibit?

☐ Artistic expression and cultural diversity

☐ The excitement of traveling

☐ The importance of technology

☐ The fun of playing games

8.34) What do the children learn from organizing the exhibit?

☐ Basic computer skills

☐ Tips for gardening

☐ How to cook

☐ About different art forms and community pride

8.35) What is the outcome of their art exhibit project?

☐ It unites the community and gains wide attention

☐ They build a new playground

☐ They start a sports club

☐ It is cancelled due to rain

In the historic town of Old Oak, a young boy named Alex started a project to document the stories of the town's oldest trees. He interviewed local experts and researched in the town library, learning about the trees' significance and history. Alex discovered stories of ancient events, legends, and the trees' roles in the community. His project highlighted the importance of nature in local heritage and sparked a town-wide initiative to preserve these natural landmarks.

8.36) What is the focus of Alex's project in Old Oak?

☐ Organizing a community festival

☐ Documenting stories of the town's oldest trees

☐ Building a treehouse

☐ Playing sports in the local park

ALEXANDER-GRACE EDUCATION

8.37) How does the research in the town library add to the story?

☐ It serves as a setting for a celebration

☐ It is a location for Alex to meet friends

☐ As a place for Alex to rest

☐ It provides historical information about the trees

8.38) What theme emerges from Alex's documentation of the trees?

☐ The fun of camping

☐ The excitement of outdoor sports

☐ The importance of technology

☐ The connection between nature and local heritage

8.39) What does Alex learn from his project?

☐ Tips for gardening

☐ Basics of computer programming

☐ The significance of trees in the town's history

☐ How to cook

8.40) What is the impact of Alex's project on the town?

☐ It is ignored by the residents

☐ It leads to a new construction project

☐ It inspires a preservation initiative for the trees

☐ It starts a sports league

Topic 8 – Answers

Question Number	Answer	Explanation
8.1	The discovery of a secret garden	The main idea of the story is the children's discovery and transformation of a secret garden.
8.2	As the main destination of the children's adventure	The secret garden is the key destination and focus of the children's adventure.
8.3	Friendship and adventure	The story explores themes of friendship, courage, and the joy of discovery through the children's journey.
8.4	Solving riddles	The children face the challenge of solving riddles to find and restore the garden.
8.5	They transform the garden	The outcome is that the children find and transform the garden into a beautiful space for everyone.
8.6	Organizing a neighborhood cleanup	Lily's story focuses on her and her friends organizing a cleanup of their local park.
8.7	It motivates the cleanup effort	The park's littered condition motivates Lily and her friends to take action and clean it up.
8.8	Environmental conservation and community	The story explores themes of environmental conservation and the impact of community involvement.
8.9	Coordinating the event	Lily and her friends face the challenge of coordinating the cleanup event and motivating others.
8.10	The successful cleanup of the park	Their efforts result in the successful cleanup and revitalization of the park.
8.11	Learning about local wildlife	The students' project is centered on learning about local wildlife through nature hikes and observation.
8.12	They provide opportunities for wildlife observation	The nature hikes are crucial for the students to observe and learn about wildlife in their natural habitats.
8.13	Wildlife diversity and habitat preservation	The theme of wildlife diversity and the importance of preserving their habitats is highlighted.
8.14	Identifying animal tracks and behaviors	The students encounter challenges in identifying animal tracks and understanding animal behavior.
8.15	A deeper appreciation for nature	The outcome is a deeper appreciation and understanding of nature and environmental stewardship.
8.16	Exploring sea life and learning about marine creatures	The primary focus is on exploring sea life and learning about different marine creatures at the aquarium.
8.17	It educates them about marine habitats and behaviors	Observing marine creatures adds educational value, teaching the children about marine life and their habitats.
8.18	The complexity of marine ecosystems and conservation	The story emphasizes the complexity of marine ecosystems and the importance of conservation efforts.

8.19	Understanding ecosystems and pollution's impact	The children face challenges in grasping the complexity of ecosystems and how pollution affects marine life.
8.20	Increased interest in marine biology and conservation	The visit leads to a heightened interest in marine biology and a desire to protect ocean life.
8.21	Exploring an old library and learning from books	Tim's story revolves around his discovery of an old library and learning from its vast collection of books.
8.22	It initiates Tim's journey of learning and discovery	The discovery of the library is the starting point for Tim's exploration and learning journey.
8.23	The value of knowledge and learning	The theme of the story is the power of knowledge and the joy of learning from books.
8.24	About history, science, and cultures	Tim learns about a wide range of subjects, including history, science, and various cultures.
8.25	It becomes a center for learning for Tim and his friends	Tim's discovery leads to the library becoming a hub of learning and adventure for him and his friends.
8.26	Learning about local history	The main subject of the project is learning about the local history of Riverview.
8.27	They help uncover the town's past	Visits to historical landmarks contribute by helping the friends uncover stories of the town's past.
8.28	The richness of local history and its impact	The theme of the project is the exploration of local history and its influence on the present.
8.29	Stories of the town's founding and notable figures	The friends learn about the town's founding, important events, and notable historical figures.
8.30	A school presentation inspiring interest in history	The outcome is a school presentation that sparks interest in local history among peers.
8.31	Creating an art exhibit	The central activity is creating an art exhibit that showcases the community's culture.
8.32	It showcases the community's culture	The artwork contributes by showcasing the diverse backgrounds and traditions of the community.
8.33	Artistic expression and cultural diversity	The theme highlighted is the importance of artistic expression and recognizing cultural diversity.
8.34	About different art forms and community pride	Organizing the exhibit teaches the children about various art forms and instills community pride.
8.35	It unites the community and gains wide attention	The art exhibit project unites the community and draws attention from a wider audience.
8.36	Documenting stories of the town's oldest trees	Alex's project focuses on documenting the history and stories of Old Oak's oldest trees.
8.37	It provides historical information about the trees	Research in the town library adds depth to the story by providing historical context about the trees.
8.38	The connection between nature and local heritage	The theme emerging is the significance of nature in the town's history and local heritage.
8.39	The significance of trees in the town's history	Alex learns about the historical and cultural importance of the town's oldest trees.
8.40	It inspires a preservation initiative for the trees	Alex's project leads to a town-wide initiative to preserve these important natural landmarks.

Ready for More?

The NWEA MAP testing is adaptive. This means that if your student found these questions too tricky or too easy, they may find it useful to practice grades below or above they grade they are in. This will expose students to new concepts and ideas, giving them a better chance at scoring higher in tests.

Alexander-Grace Education produces books covering Mathematics, Sciences, and English, to help your student maximize their potential in these areas.

For errata, please email
alexandergraceeducation@gmail.com

Made in the USA
Columbia, SC
31 March 2025

55978446R00065